A Comparison of Twelve Technical Trading Systems

Traders Press, Inc.®
PO Box 6206
Greenville, SC 29606

Serving Traders Since 1975
http://www.traderspress.com

Louis P. Lukac
B. Wade Brorsen
Scott H. Irwin

This publication is designed to provide accurate and authoritative information with regard to the subject matter covered. It is sold with the understanding that the publisher is not engaged in rendering legal, accounting, or other professional advice. If legal advice or other expert assistance is required, the services of a competent professional person should be sought. No representation is made that the methods presented in this book are or will be profitable. Any person acting on the ideas herein is responsible for his own actions, and acts at his own risk.

ISBN: 0-934380-18-X

Layout and Cover Design by: Teresa Darty Alligood
Traders Press, Inc.®

Traders Press, Inc.®
PO Box 6206
Greenville, SC 29606

Serving Traders Since 1975
http://www.traderspress.com

Autobiographical Sketch
Louis Lukac

Louis Lukac is founder and President of Wizard Trading Inc. a 15 year old alternative investment management firm registered as a commodity trading advisor specializing in managed futures investing. Mr. Lukac has been involved in the research, development, testing and implementation of trading strategies in the global futures/derivatives markets for over 18 years. Prior to Wizard, he was the Assistant Director and then the Director of Futures/Derivatives Research for Prudential Securities Incorporated in New York where he oversaw market analysts and trading floor staff, reviewed all proprietary research reports and developed and implemented hedging strategies for clients of the firm. Mr. Lukac was also the Vice President of Investment Services and Research Director for Dunn and Hargitt Investment Management, Inc., a registered commodity trading advisor and commodity pool operator. He has a B.S. in Management/Finance and an M.S. in Agricultural Economics, both from Purdue University in West Lafayette, IN. Mr. Lukac has served as President and Director of the Futures Industry Association's Futures Research Division, Chicago Chapter. His research on trading system development and portfolio analysis has been published in journals such as Applied Economics, Financial Review, Journal of Futures Markets, Stock & Commodities Magazine, and Futures Magazine.

Louis Lukac first became interested in technical systems as a junior in an undergraduate investments course at Purdue. After receiving his Bachelors degree in Management/Finance, his curiosity in this area of research led him to Wade Brorsen and Scott Irwin in the Agricultural Economics Department at Purdue. Wade Brorsen became his major professor and Scott Irwin provided valuable guidance as a Ph.D. graduate student. The paper "A Comparison of Twelve Technical Trading Systems with Market Efficiency Implications," resulted fro Louis Lukac's M.S. thesis.

Autobiographical Sketch

B. Wade Brorsen is an associate professor in the Department of Agricultural Economics at Purdue University. He has published over 15 academic journal articles on various aspects of futures markets. He has also published several trade articles together with Louis Lukac and Scott Irwin. His journal articles on futures markets have appeared in <u>Journal of Futures Markets</u>, <u>Review of Research in Futures Markets</u>, <u>Journal of Financial & Quantitative Analysis</u>, and others. The trade articles were in <u>Futures</u> and <u>Technical Analysis of Stocks & Commodities</u>. Dr. Brorsen teaches a Ph.D. course in econometrics--advanced statistical techniques for economists.

The paper, "A Comparison of Twelve Technical Trading Systems with Market Efficiency Implications," resulted from Louis Lukac's M.S. thesis. Dr. Brorsen served as Louis Lukac's thesis advisor. Scott Irwin was a Ph.D. graduate student. Scott Irwin had completed a similar, though much less comprehensive study for his M.S. thesis. Louis spent many hours at a computer terminal to obtain the results.

Biography of Scott H. Irwin

Scott H. Irwin grew up on a grain and livestock farm in west central Iowa. In 1980, he earned the Bachelor of Science Degree in Agricultural Business from Iowa State University. In 1983, he received the Master of Science in Agricultural Economics at Purdue University. In 1986, he received the Doctor of Philosopy with a major in agricultural economics from Purdue University. Dr. Irwin joined the faculty of The Ohio State University in 1985. Currently, he is an Associate Professor in the Department of Agricultural Economics and Rural Sociology. His research interests are in the area of commodity futures and options markets and commodity price analysis. Recent research projects have investigated the reaction of live hog futures prices to the release of USDA Hogs and Pigs Reports and the accuracy of time series models in forecasting soybean complex prices.

Publisher's Foreword

This superlative piece of technical research was the thesis for Louis Lukac's Masters degree at Purdue University. When I first discovered it in the late 1980's, it was "drawing dust" in the archives of the library at Purdue, and was not generally known or available to the thousands of traders who would find this material valuable in their technical trading research. Although the research herein is now two decades old, it is still of value to those interested in systems research and development. In fact, my good friend Wayne Griffith, well-known in trading systems circles as the developer of "Anticipation," recently advised me that he was specifically interested in old systems which have been around for a long time, on the premise that if systems which worked years ago still continued to work in the interim, this was evidence of their "staying power," which is the hallmark of a truly good system, which has stood the test of time. Those interested in systems research will want to update the research originally published in this material. The systems which have continued to perform during the 20 year interim since this document was originally released will be of particular interest.

I am deeply grateful to the three individuals involved in the creation of this research (Messrs. Lukac, Brorsen, and Irwin) for their permission to reprint and distribute it.

Edward Dobson

Edward D. Dobson, President   **November 17, 2004**
Traders Press, Inc.®
Greenville, SC

A COMPARISON OF TWELVE TECHNICAL TRADING SYSTEMS WITH MARKET EFFICIENCY IMPLICATIONS

Many researchers have simulated trading to determine if profits are attainable using trading systems. The main objective of previous research was to test market efficiency, defined by Fama as a market in which prices fully reflect all available information, or to test market disequilibrium models (Nawrocki). Numerous studies have found profits from trading futures contracts by a pre-specified rule. Studies have analyzed grain contracts (Houthakker; Smidt; Stevenson and Bear) live-stock contracts (Leuthold; Peterson and Leuthold), as well as financials (Dale and Workman). These studies have found technical analysis to be profitable. However, these studies were generally based on short time spans as well as a small number of commodities.

Irwin and Uhrig, as well as Irwin and Brorsen (1984), used many contracts with long time spans. Additionally, both studies used the concept of a pre-test or optimization of the trading systems to develop optimized systems and out-of-sample results. Equally unique, both studies generated commodity portfolio returns to measure trading profits. This approach corresponds to how a commodity pool actually trades and thus simulated returns can be compared to observed returns. However, Irwin and Brorsen's study simulated only one system and Irwin and Uhrig simulated out-of-sample results for just four systems over a short period using primarily agricultural commodities. This would suggest that simulating more systems out-of-sample for a longer period and using a diversified portfolio of not only agricultural commodities but currencies, metals and financials as well would improve on previous tests of the usefulness of technical analysis. In addition, few studies have adjusted trading system returns for risk. More powerful tests of market efficiency should account for risk.

The only information most past studies have provided traders about what system(s) to use was the mean and variance of returns. Risk reduction may be possible by diversifying across a portfolio of systems. With a portfolio of systems, preferred mixes of systems could be determined to reduce a trader's risk exposure. Equally important would be to determine the preferred single system, given a trader's level of risk aversion. This type of information would be important to traders who are concerned about limiting their risk. Also, most past studies only examined one or two technical trading systems.

Past studies have contributed valuable information about commodity trading systems. But, empirical research concerning risk adjusted market efficiency tests and preferred trading system(s) is nearly void. The purpose of this study is to determine if profits are attainable by technical trading systems and to determine the preferred technical trading system(s) a trader would want to use.

MARKET EFFICIENCY

The ability of technical trading systems to generate profits has important implications for market efficiency and therefore for users of futures markets. Prices in an efficient market should reflect the underlying supply and demand conditions (fundamentals) quickly and accurately. Firms, who base their current and future production decisions on market prices, need market prices that are both timely and accurate. Inefficient market signals will result in inefficient firm decisions. Profits to technical trading systems may indicate markets are not reflecting the fundamentals quickly and accurately.

Many different theories have been developed to study market efficiency (Fama; Samuelson). Fama defined an efficient market as one where prices fully reflect all available information. Jensen (1978) has offered a similar definition which states a market is efficient with respect to an information set if it is impossible to make economic profits by trading on the basis of the information set. The efficient market hypothesis is the basis for the dominant model used to explain the behavior of speculative prices. The efficient market hypothesis has been defined for three different levels or sets of information. The weak form includes only past prices in the information set. The semi-strong form information set includes all information that is publicly available while the strong form information set includes all information known to anyone. Since technical trading systems only use past prices, they provide a test of weak form market efficiency.

The zero economic profits implied by the efficient market hypothesis are meant to be risk adjusted returns net of all costs (Jensen, 1978). Earlier market models, such as the general Martingale market model implied a zero return in speculative markets under the assumptions of zero transactions and storage costs and risk neutral traders. Jensen's (1978) definition is more restrictive, and should provide a stronger test of market efficiency. Therefore, an alternative weak form efficiency test would be whether a trading system could earn a return above a return for risk. One difficulty with such a test is defining the "normal" return for risk (Brorsen and Irwin).

Furthermore Beja and Goldman suggested a disequilibrium pricing model which theoretically allows for profitable technical trading. Beja and Goldman (p. 235) suggest, "... it is intuitively inconceivable that a man-made institution (such as a market) could be so mechanically perfect that all (price) discrepancies would be totally annihilated before they can be observed." Therefore prices will be slow to reflect information about supply and demand factors (fundamentals). The information is not acted on instantly because of transaction costs, taxes, cost of acquiring and evaluating information, and poor methods and sources for obtaining information. Without instantaneous adjustment, a market is in short run disequilibrium and speculation based solely on the price trend may be profitable as the market moves toward equilibrium. Thus, the use of technical trading systems which forecast price trends may play an essential role in short-run speculation.

The preceding discussion suggests two testable hypotheses concerning futures market efficiency. The first hypothesis is no trading system could produce positive economic profits. A second nested hypothesis is that even if returns are positive, they are not above a return to risk. This paper uses a framework suggested by Jensen (1968) to adjust returns for risk. This offers a more powerful test of market efficiency using trading systems.

Studies of futures market efficiency using trading systems are numerous (e.g., Peterson and Leuthold; Irwin and Uhrig). Conclusions reached from these studies could be questioned because generally short time spans are chosen, few trading systems and commodities are used and no adjustment for risk is made. This study corrects for these shortcomings.

DATA AND PROCEDURE

The methods are presented in this section. The general trading model is introduced first, followed by the trading systems and the portfolio model. Next, the portfolio of commodities, the data, and market efficiency tests are explained. Finally, procedures to determine the preferred technical trading system(s) based on risk and expected return are introduced.

Trading Model

The trading model is a computer program which simulates the trading of the technical trading systems. This model can simulate trading of nearly any type of objective technical trading system. The model keeps track of important criteria such as profits and losses, number of trades, average profit per trade. The model is used to generate optimal parameters for each system and commodity.

Input

A continuous price series of daily futures prices is needed to simulate trading. One method widely used by researchers (Smidt; Peterson, and Leuthold; Stevenson and Bear) is to use one contract, i.e., the December corn contract, as a single representative proxy of futures prices and then create a string of contracts to represent the continuous price series. Using December corn, this would mean stringing together December 1975, December 1976, ..., December 1984 to make the price series. Each contract would be traded for its calendar year.

The simulation model is intended to replicate how actual traders use trading systems. Price series constructed of successive single contracts are a poor approximation of the actual use of technical trading systems. Traders usually hold positions only in the "nearby" contract because of liquidity costs. A more representative approach uses the concept of a dominant contract (Dale and Workman; Irwin and Uhrig; and Irwin and Brorsen, 1984). Dale and Workman used this method in their study which started with the March 1976 T-bill futures contract. This contract was used until the June 1976 contract became dominant, which was used until the September 1976 contract became dominant, etc. Thus the most current or nearby contract is used for the construction of the continuous price series.

A problem arising from the use of dominant futures contracts is that the price difference between the old dominant contract and new dominant contract at the time of roll-over may be large enough to create a discontinuous break in the price series, thus a false signal. A solution to these discontinuous breaks adopted by Irwin and Uhrig and practiced by Dunn involves comparing the signals given by the trading system from the old dominant contract and the new dominant contract. The procedure is as follows: 1) On the roll-over day the position (long, short, neutral) given by the trading system using price data from the old dominant contract is compared to the position given by the trading system using price data from the new dominant contract; 2) If the positions differ, the new position or signal is taken from the new dominant contract.

Transaction Costs and Assumptions

Transaction costs are considered in two parts. One is the commission charged for each trade. A second transaction cost is known as skid error and is defined as the difference between the price at which an order to buy or sell on an open or close would actually have been filled and the quoted price for a market opening or closing in an historical price series.

The trading model accounts for commission costs by subtracting from the gross profits or losses of a trading system an estimated commission for each trade including the roll-over trade from the switching of dominant contracts. Skid error has been considered important by Barker and Dunn. Mandlebrot argued Alexander's results were biased because he did not account for skid error. Fama and Blume also expressed concern about skid error resulting in biased results. Because many of the trading systems used in this study assume that if a buy or sell signal is generated today and action is to be taken on today's close or the next day's open, skid error can significantly influence the results. Barker and Dunn offer the simplest method to account for this error. They use an oversized commission such as double the commission cost. This method was used in the trading model, and a $100.00 commission charge assessed for each trade (initial and offsetting position) thus all profits are conservatively estimated and closer to actual trading returns.

Several other assumptions underlie the trading model. First, a position is not entered or exited when the contract's opening price is up or down the allowable limit for the day. This procedure was adopted because a trader could not trade on limit days. Second, when generating optimal parameters, all trading is on a one contract basis, i.e., only one contract is traded at a time. Third, no pyramiding of positions is allowed. Finally, any drawdown in equity from losses is assumed to be met with additional capital and any profits are assumed to be withdrawn.

Portfolio Model

The individual commodity returns and aggregate portfolio returns for each system are generated by a portfolio model that uses the optimal parameters for each trading system and commodity. The portfolio model trades several different commodities at the same time, similar to how actual trading is done by futures funds.

The portfolio model assumes equal dollar amounts are invested in margins for each commodity. Aggregate portfolio returns are calculated using the appropriate weights for the individual commodity returns. Commodity percent returns are calculated assuming 30% of total funds is invested in initial margins and 70% is held back for potential margin calls. Margins vary by commodity, but are assumed to be about 10% of contract value (less for the financials). For example, a trader who invested $1,000 would use $300 for initial margins and hold back $700 for potential margin calls. If profits were $100 over the period, then the percent return would be 10%.

This study uses the total investment (initial margins plus reserve for margin calls) to calculate percentage returns. An alternative approach is to express returns as a percent of contract value. This alternative would generate percent returns one-third as large as the total investment method. Another alternative would be to calculate returns as a percent of initial margins. This method would generate returns three and one-third times higher than the total investment method. Thus, percent returns using alternative approaches can easily be calculated from the results presented here.

Several assumptions which hold for the trading model also hold for the portfolio model. First, no trading is allowed on limit days. Second, no pyramiding of profits or positions is allowed (i.e., no rein-vestment of profits). Finally, any drawdown in equity from losses is assumed to be met with additional capital and commissions are $100 per round turn trade.

Technical Trading Systems

The methodical buying and selling of futures contracts based on some pre-specified trading rule without regard to underlying fundamen-tals constitutes a technical trading system. Numerous trading systems have been suggested. The selection of the trading system is crucial to the objectives of this study because they must closely represent the systems used by traders.

After conversations with traders who use technical trading systems, as well as a review of previous studies and books (Barker; Wilder; New Concepts; Kaufman; Irwin and Uhrig), twelve trading systems were selected. The trading systems represent price channels, moving aver-ages, and momentum oscillators, as well as systems with trailing stops and combination systems. The trading systems selected for this study are presented in Appendix A. These systems are 1) Close Channel (CNL), 2) L-S-O Price Channel (LSO), 3) MII Price Channel (MII), 4) Directional Indicator (DRI), 5) Directional Movement (DRM), 6) Range Quotient (RNQ), 7) Reference Deviation (REF), 8) Moving Average with Percentage Price Band (MAB), 9) Dual Moving Average Crossover (DMC), 10) Parabolic Time/Price (PAR), 11) Directional Movement-Parabolic Combination (DRP), and 12) Alexander's Filter Rule (ALX).

These systems were selected to be representative of the various types of systems that have been suggested. They should not, however, be considered equal in importance. A trader interviewed by Laing argued the managers of most futures funds use the dual moving average crossover system, while Dunn argues various price channel systems are popular. Both argued that oscillators are rarely used as the sole basis of trading. Brorsen and Irwin (1986) found that several fund managers have recently adopted some type of a combination system. The systems traders actually use are more likely to be profitable and thus they are the ones that should provide a stronger test of market efficiency.

Optimization Method

Optimization refers to a method of determining the parameters for the trading systems. Technical trading systems can be either adaptive, taking advantage of some past information, or non-adaptive, trading without regard to previous information. Adaptive trading systems alter current parameters based upon previous performance of the parameters, thus the system adapts to changes by changing parameters. The selection of an optimal parameter (parameter which generates the highest return), whether by adaptive or non-adaptive means is referred to as optimizing the system. Most previous research (Stevenson and Bear; Smidt; Peterson and Leuthold) used non-adaptive procedures and did not simulate trading over a period different than the optimization period. Taylor and Praetz have argued that trading system profits obtained by optimizing the choice of parameter on past data are meaningless. The correct procedure is to use part of the available data to help choose the parameter and then to assess the rule upon the remaining data, using only the chosen parameter. Simulating the chosen parameter upon the remaining data insures all trading results are out-of-sample and closer to actual trading profits. This is the approach taken in this study.

Nawrocki, Martell and Philippatos, Irwin and Uhrig, and Irwin and Brorsen (1984) have all used adaptive trading systems, thus pre-testing parameters on previous price data to generate the optimal parameter used for trading on current prices. A pre-test strategy used by Irwin and Brorsen is a three year re-optimization approach, in which each year's optimal parameter is based on the parameters performance over the previous three years. Specifically, for each commodity, trading is simulated by each system over three years over a range of parameters. The range of parameters is limited because of limits on computer resources. Thus the testing of every value between a given range was not possible. The parameter yielding the highest profit over the three year optimization period is then used for the subsequent year. At the end of that year, the system is re-optimized over the previous three years of trading, thus generating a new optimal parameter used for the next year of trading. This is the approach used in this study. Since the systems are adaptive and results out-of-sample, the simulation corresponds closer to how traders actually use technical systems, a crucial issue for studying profitability.

Data

To provide a more powerful test of market efficiency, a diversified portfolio of twelve highly traded commodities, metals, and financials as chosen (Table 1). All the data used for this study are from 1975

Table 1. Commodities, Trading Periods, and Exchanges for Simulation.

Commodity	Trading Period	Exchange
Corn	1975-1984	CBT
Cocoa	1975-1984	CSCE
Copper	1975-1984	CMX
Live Cattle	1975-1984	CME
Lumber	1975-1984	CME
Pork Bellies	1975-1984	CME
Soybeans	1975-1984	CBT
Silver (N.Y.)	1975-1984	CMX
Sugar	1975-1984	CSCE
U.S. Treasury Bills	1976-1984	IMM
British Pound	1977-1984	IMM
Deutsche Mark	1977-1984	IMM

[a] CBT — Chicago Board of Trade

CSCE — Coffee, Sugar, Cocoa Exchange, Incorporated

CME — Chicago Mercantile Exchange

IMM — International Monetary Market of Chicago Mercantile Exchange

CMX — Commodity Exchange, New York

through 1984. This avoids 1973 and 1974 when agricultural markets experienced structural change and oil price shocks disrupted markets. However, since the Deutsche Mark, British Pound, and U.S. Treasury Bills did not start trading until 1977, 1977, and 1976, respectively, these three contracts are traded as soon as three years of data are available. Most of the profits in Irwin and Uhrig's study came in the period 1973 through 1977. They and others (Hieronymus) explained the occurrence of profitable periods with the argument that due to extraordinary conditions traders could not efficiently assess market conditions and thus the disequilibrium resulted in profits to technical systems. Because of the optimization method, this study has actual trading only over the 1978 through 1984 period (1975 through 1977 are used to generate the optimal parameters for 1978). Thus, the time period 1973-77, during which past research strongly suggests futures markets were inefficient because of special circumstances, is avoided. Furthermore, this time frame prevented any pre-testing in terms of selection of the systems, thus any bias in the test for efficiency in the selection of the systems is lessened.

Market Efficiency Tests

A controversy surrounding trading system returns is whether sufficient profits exist to refute Fama's definition of weak form efficiency. Peterson and Leuthold used a z-statistic to test the null hypothesis that mean gross profits from any trading system were equal to zero. They used a two-tailed test assuming that significantly negative returns could have been positive if the system's trading criteria were reversed. However, the systems used in this study are designed to trade by set criteria. Therefore to reverse this set of criteria would not correspond to how a trader would actually use the system. Furthermore, Peterson and Leuthold did not subtract transaction costs. This study subtracts transaction costs, therefore a one-tailed test is appropriate.

This study uses an approach similar to Peterson and Leuthold. However, this study tests for positive returns using a monthly return from a portfolio of commodities and using monthly returns from each market. Even though it is individual markets which are either efficient or inefficient, the portfolio returns provide an efficiency test across all markets and thus may be a more powerful test of market efficiency. The hypotheses in either case are

$$H_0: \quad MMR = 0$$

$$H_1: \quad MMR > 0$$

where MMR is the mean monthly portfolio or market return from a technical trading system.

The statistical test selected to test the null hypothesis is

$$(1) \quad t = \frac{\bar{X} - X_0}{S/n}$$

where $\bar{X}$ is the MMR from a given trading system, X_0 is the expected MMR (zero in this case), S is the standard deviation of monthly returns from a given system and n is the total number of months.

The use of a t-statistic assumes that the underlying distribution of monthly returns have a normal and independent distribution. However, Taylor argues, "The distribution of the return from a filter strategy under the null hypothesis of an efficient market is not known, so that proper significance tests are impossible." But, even if daily prices are not distributed normally, aggregate portfolio or market returns from trading systems may be normally distributed and thus, t-tests may be appropriate.

Gardner points out the use of a t-statistic may overstate the significance of the results if returns are positively autocorrelated. Gardner argues that if positive autocorrelation exists, the number of observations is actually overstated, and thus significance levels may be overstated.

This study addresses both potential shortcomings of using a t-statistic. First a Kolmogorov-Smirnov (KS) test is performed to test the distribution of monthly returns for normality (Shannon). Second, first order autocorrelation coefficients are calculated to determine if monthly returns are positively autocorrelated, thus significance levels overstated. Both the KS test and first order autocorrelation test address the possible shortcomings of the use of a t-statistic expressed by previous researchers.

Another problem with using a t-test to test economic efficiency is that all traders are assumed risk neutral, thus a return significantly above zero is considered evidence against efficiency. Panton, Danthine, Leroy, and others have relaxed this assumption by assuming, more realistically, that traders are risk averse and that in an economically efficient market, traders could not obtain a profit above a return to risk. This involves analyzing the relationship between the riskiness of returns and the risk aversion of investors. The procedure used is similar to Jensen's test of market efficiency, which he used to test efficiency in the security market.

The Jensen test is based on the Capital Asset Pricing Model (CAPM). The CAPM implies

$$(2) \quad E(R_i) = R_F + [E(R_m) - R_F]B_i$$

where $E(R_i)$ is the expected return on asset i, R_F is the risk free rate, $E(R_m)$ is expected rate of return on total wealth or market portfolio and B_i is the relative risk or systematic risk of asset i given by

$$(3) \quad B_i = \frac{COV(R_i, R_m)}{\sigma^2_{R_m}}$$

where $\sigma^2_{R_m}$ is the variance of the market portfolio. Equation (2) can be rewritten as:

$$(4) \quad E(R_i) - R_F = [E(R_m) - R_F]B_i$$

In this study $E(R_i)$ is the monthly return of system i, R_F is Ibbotson Associates data on returns from 30-day U.S. Treasury Bills, and $E(R_m)$ is represented by the returns to the Standard & Poor's 500 Stock Index as computed by Ibbotson Associates. However, since the capital invested in margins, as well as that held for margin calls, could have been simultaneously invested in 30-day U.S. Treasury Bills, R_F did not need to be subtracted from $E(R_i)$ in this study.

One difficulty in applying this framework to commodity markets is selecting the appropriate measure of the return to wealth or market return. Dusak, while applying capital market theory to test for commodity market risk premiums, used the Standard and Poor Index of 500 major common stocks (S&P 500) as a proxy. Carter, Rausser, and Schmitz criticized Dusak for this selection and used an index composed of the S&P 500 and the Dow Jones Commodity Futures Index, each weighted at 50%. However, Marcus, as well as Baxter, Conine, and Tamarkin, argued the futures portion of this index was overweighted. Baxter, Conine and Tamarkin constructed a market return index of 93.7% S&P 500 and 6.3% Dow Jones Commodity Cash Index which yielded the same conclusion as Dusak reached. Black argued, "To the extent that stocks of commodities are held by corporations, they are implicitly included in the market portfolio." This study uses the S&P 500 because this measure seems to incorporate commodities as suggested by Black.

Letting $E(R_m) - R_F$ equal R_i^* and $E(R_m - R_F)$ equal R_m^* then (4) can be written as a linear regression model:

$$(5) \quad R_i^* = a_i + B_i R_m^* + e_i$$

where the usual assumptions of the linear regression model are assumed to hold.

The test of market efficiency is to test the intercept term a_i to determine if it is above zero, thus determine if returns exist above returns to risk. This approach allows the test of market efficiency with regard to risk using each system's monthly returns as potential returns from futures markets. If significantly positive intercepts are found, inefficiency may exist.

Selection of Preferred System(s)

Traders and users of technical trading systems are concerned about risk. One way traders have previously reduced risk is to trade more than one commodity. Another approach is to diversify across systems to reduce risk. This method involves analysis of system returns and risk. This study examines two measures to aid in differentiating among systems on the basis of both risk and return.

One method which accounts for return and risk is based on modern portfolio theory (Markowitz). This framework defines a portfolio as efficient if it 1) offers a higher expected return than any other portfolio having the same risk, and 2) offers a lower level of risk than any other portfolio having the same expected rate of return (Bellemore, et al.). The portfolio in this case is the twelve trading systems. One mathematical means of applying the portfolio selection criteria is quadratic programming. Specifically:

$$(6) \quad \text{Minimize:} \quad V = \sum_{i=1}^{N} \sum_{j=1}^{N} \sigma_{ij} X_i X_j$$

$$\text{Subject to:} \quad E = \sum_{i=1}^{N} X_i U_i$$

$$X_i \geq 0 \text{ for } i = 1, \ldots, N$$

$$\sum_{i=1}^{N} X_i = 1$$

where V is the variance of the returns from the N trading system portfolio, σ_{ij} is the variance of returns to system i if i = j or the covariance between returns to system i and j if i ≠ j, X_i and X_j are weights or the proportion of the portfolio allocated to systems i and j. E is the expected return from the portfolio and U_i is the average monthly return from system i. To generate an efficient set of systems, E is varied from zero to a maximum monthly return. This procedure generates weights or proportions in which to allocate resources to each system thus providing strategies to minimize risk while obtaining a certain level of return.

A further measure to aid in differentiating among the twelve systems is stochastic dominance. This procedure ranks distributions based on an investors risk preference (Meyer). Risk averse investors' preference among distributions is represented by $r(x) = U''(x)/U'(x)$, where x

is income or wealth and U'(x) and U"(x) are the first and second deriva-
tives of the utility function. Meyer considers the group of investors
whose preferences are represented by r(x) satisfying

(7) $r_1(x) \leq r(x) \leq r_2(x)$, for all $X > 0$

where $r_1(x)$ and $r_x(x)$ are given known functions. Distributions are then
ranked for all investors whose risk preferences fall in the range
defined by (7).

This method provides a ranking of systems with regard to risk preference of the investor. One difficulty in applying Meyer's procedure is
specifying $r_1(x)$ and $r_2(x)$, the interval of risk preferences. Kramer
and Pope, King and Robinson and Meyer have all used series of intervals
based on different criteria. This study uses the range used by Brorsen
and Irwin because the data used had similar means and standard devia-
tions. The interval used to compare the monthly returns of the twelve
trading systems is [-0.1, 0.1]. Brorsen and Irwin argue that this range
should include the majority of investors.

RESULTS AND IMPLICATIONS

All the results of this study are from optimized trading systems.
Optimal is defined as the trading system parameters, i.e. (Days,
Percent, etc.) that yielded the highest profit over the preceding three
years, hence the term three year reoptimization. The simulated returns
were generated from these optimal parameters. These optimal parameters
are presented in Appendix B (Tables A.1 through A.13 for each trading
system, each trading year, and each commodity. Optimal parameters are
also included for 1985 so that they could be used in further research.

Martingale Efficient Markets Model Test

The test of the Martingale efficient markets model assumes normality of the underlying distribution of returns. Table 2 presents the
results of the Kolmogorov-Smirnov test for normality of aggregate
monthly returns from all twelve systems. In each case normality is not
rejected. Furthermore Gardner suggested if returns from trading systems
were positively autocorrelated, significance levels of statistical tests
may be overstated. Results in Table 3 indicate negative autocorrelation
in all twelve of the system's monthly aggregate returns. Four of the
coefficients are significantly negative at the 10 percent level. This
would suggest that the confidence levels of the one tailed test statis-
tic for these four systems are more likely to be understated than overstated. Thus the t-tests used here may be conservative.

Monthly returns for each system are presented in Table 4. Four out
of the twelve systems had significant (10 percent level or less) mean
monthly aggregate returns. These systems are the channel (CNL), directional parabolic (DRP), MII price channel (MII), and the dual moving

Table 2. Kolmogorov-Smirnov Test for Normality of Monthly Aggregate
Returns, All Twelve Systems, 1978-1984.[a]

System	Test Statistic[b]
Channel	.0572
Parabolic	.0753
Directional Movement	.0533
Range Quotient	.0838
Directional Parabolic	.0741
MII Price Channel	.0695
L-S-O Price Channel	.0660
Reference Deviation	.0678
Dual Moving Average Crossover	.0677
Directional Indicator	.0502
Moving Average w/% Price Band	.0596
Alexander's Filter Rule	.0552

[a] Aggregated returns across all commodities.

[b] None are significant at the .10 level or less.

Table 3. Autocorrelation Coefficients of Monthly Returns for All Twelve
          Systems, 1978-1984.

Trading System[a]	Autocorrelation Coefficient[b]	Associated t-value
CHL	-.043	-.3941
PAR	-.031	-.2841
DRM	-.141	-1.2923
RNQ	-.065	-.5957
DRP	-.076	-.6966
MII	-.178*	-1.6314
LSO	-.132	-1.2098
REF	-.175*	-1.6039
DMC	-.322***	-2.9512
DRI	-.069	-.6324
MAB	-.104	-.9532
ALX	-.254**	-2.3279

[a] CHL = Channel   LSO = L-S-O Price Channel
    PAR = Parabolic   REF = Reference Deviation
    DRM = Directional Movement DMC = Dual Moving Average Crossover
    RNQ = Range Quotient   DRI = Directional Indicator
    DRP = Directional Parabolic MAB = Moving Average w/% Price Band
    MII = MII Price Channel   ALX = Alexander's Filter Rule

[b] Significance levels denoted by * at .10 level, ** at .025 level, and
*** at .005 level.

Table 4. Mean, t-value, Standard Deviation, Minimum, and Maximum of
Monthly Portfolio Returns for All Twelve Systems, 1978-1984.

Trading System[a]	Mean % Return[b,c]	t-values	Standard Deviation	Minimum % Return	Maximum % Return
CHL	2.78**	1.99	12.81	-23.57	36.71
PAR	.30	.23	11.78	-34.65	34.48
DRM	1.06	.76	12.87	-33.81	34.09
RNQ	-6.60	-3.82	15.84	-47.72	28.67
DRP	2.65*	1.52	16.04	-33.75	50.65
MII	2.10*	1.52	12.62	-22.45	38.34
LSO	-2.61	-1.73	13.81	-33.73	36.67
REF	-2.37	-1.24	17.55	-46.17	49.05
DMC	1.89*	1.33	13.05	-23.17	47.73
DRI	-4.66	-2.49	17.18	-39.06	40.89
MAB	-5.04	-3.17	14.57	-43.26	31.65
ALX	1.08	.76	13.07	-34.13	30.28

[a] CHL - Channel   LSO - L-S-O Price Channel

   PAR - Parabolic   REF - Reference Deviation

   DRM - Directional Movement   DMC - Dual Moving Average Crossover

   RNQ - Range Quotient   DRI - Directional Indicator

   DRP - Directional Parabolic   MAB - Moving Average w/% Price Band

   MII - MII Price Channel   ALX - Alexander's Filter Rule

[b] Significance levels denoted by * at .10 level, ** at .025 level, and
*** at .005 level.

[c] Equal amounts are assumed to be invested in initial margins for each
of twelve commodities. Monthly aggregate portfolio percent returns
are calculated using the appropriate weights for the individual commodity returns.

average crossover (DMC). Many systems had large negative mean returns. Most of this can be explained by the large $100.00 commission charged per trade. Table 5 shows that annual commissions charged as a percent of equity were large. Irwin and Brorsen (1985) suggested that commissions and administrative charges as a percent of equity for public futures funds is about 19%. Thus the 27% to 56% of equity for commission charges is quite large. Gross returns suggest that most of the negative returns were due to the high commission charge assessed to account not only for transaction cost but also for skid error. Because of this high commission, the returns in this study may be conservative, thus strengthening any conclusions that reject market efficiency.

The Martingale model does not represent futures price movements from 1978 through 1984 since four out of the twelve systems simulated generated significant positive returns over the trading period. This agrees with the findings of Irwin and Uhrig. But, these results also suggest that much of the past research which considered a single system is highly dependent on the system selected.

Irwin and Brorsen (1984) using a channel system found positive simulated returns from 1961 to 1982 but, negative returns in 1983. The channel (CHL) system in this study produced positive returns every year of the simulation. The pattern indicated by Irwin and Brorsen (1984) of profits dropping off in 1982 and 1983 is supported by the results of other systems and the average for the trading year across systems (Table 6). However the CHL system produced positive profits every year. The results in Table 2 also show that 1980 was the best year for all twelve systems. A possible explanation of the difference in results of this study and Irwin and Brorsen's study is the portfolio of commodities used to generate the aggregate annual returns.

Table 7 presents annual mean returns by commodity for the period 1978 through 1984. Eight of the twelve commodities indicated some significant profits. Significant returns were found in (1) Corn by five out of twelve systems, (2) Lumber by two systems, (3) Soybeans by one system, (4) Silver by three systems, (5) Sugar by five systems, (6) British Pound by one system, (7) Deutsche mark by six systems, and (8) U.S. Treasury Bills by one system. Deutsche mark, sugar, and corn appear to be the most inefficient markets since they yielded the highest number of significant returns. Furthermore the major portion of the CHL system's positive returns came from six of the twelve commodities in the portfolio. Deleting one of these six could alter the aggregate return for the system, thus produce different results such as those of Irwin and Brorsen.

Commodity returns for every commodity by year and by trading system are presented in Appendix Table 14 through Appendix Table 25. Annual commodity returns by year and by system indicate that significant profits with respect to at least one system were possible in every commodity in at least one year. Significant profits for corn occurred in 1981 and 1982. Cocoa and copper generated significant profits in 1982 while live cattle produced significant profits in 1978 and 1979. Pork bellies had significant profits in 1978 only and lumber generated significant positive profits in 1979, 1981, and 1982. In 1980 and 1981, soybeans

Table 5. Annual Commission Charges as a Percent of Investment, Annual Portfolio Net Returns, and Annual Gross Portfolio Returns from All Twelve Systems.

Trading System[a]	Commission Charges[b]	Net Returns[c]	Gross Returns[d]
	%	%	%
CHL	32	33.4	65.4
PAR	56	3.5	59.5
DRM	41	12.8	53.8
RNQ	43	-79.2	-36.2
DRP	48	31.9	79.9
MII	40	25.2	65.2
LSO	31	-31.3	-.3
REF	28	-28.4	-.4
DMC	27	22.7	49.7
DRI	39	-55.9	-16.9
MAB	33	-60.5	-27.5
ALX	33	12.9	45.9

[a]
CHL - Channel   LSO - L-S-O Price Channel
PAR - Parabolic   REF - Reference Deviation
DRM - Directional Movement   DMC - Dual Moving Average Crossover
RNQ - Range Quotient   DRI - Directional Indicator
DRP - Directional Parabolic   MAB - Moving Average w/% Price Band
MII - MII Price Channel   ALX - Alexander's Filter Rule

[b]
As an annual percent of investment approximation. For example if a system traded a total of 500 times (round turns) over the period and commission charges are $100 per trade, then total commission charges would be $50,000. If the initial investment (this includes initial margins plus reserve for margin calls) was $100,000 then the commission charge as a percent of investment would be 50%.

[c]
Equal amounts are assumed to be invested in initial margins for each commodity. Annual aggregate portfolio returns are calculated using the appropriate weights for the individual commodity returns.

[d]
Annual returns plus commission charges.

Table 6. Annual Portfolio Returns by Year for All Twelve Systems, 1978-
          1984.[a,b]

Trading	Trading Year						
System[c]	1978	1979	1980	1981	1982	1983	1984
				%			
CHL	6.1	47.9*	81.6*	21.8	28.3	19.9	28.0
PAR	18.5	16.4	54.5	29.9	-31.7	-43.2	-19.4
DRM	29.3	21.7	92.2*	-31.6	-22.7	7.8	-7.3
RNQ	-57.2	-69.0	-9.6	-152.1	-31.2	-135.5	-100.1
DRP	34.8	63.8**	88.7*	31.0	-13.4	-20.0	38.5
MII	12.9	41.6	87.8**	54.6	-30.7	3.1	7.1
LSO	-47.1	-4.0	39.1	-55.1	-55.1	-37.6	-59.5
REF	-13.5	23.3	53.2	-85.2	2.0	-109.6	-69.2
DMC	17.6	26.8	85.4*	5.9	22.9	1.9	-1.6
DRI	-60.7	-15.4	46.3	-108.1	-114.4	-105.3	-34.0
MAB	-38.0	-44.3	-7.7	-114.4	-91.1	-81.8	-45.7
ALX	28.3	38.6	82.6*	-34.4	-8.2	-2.0	-14.4
AVERAGE	-5.8	12.3	57.8	-36.5	-28.8	-41.9	-23.1

[a] Equal amounts are assumed to be invested in initial margins for each
commodity. Annual aggregate portfolio percent returns are calculated
using the appropriate weights for the individual commodity returns.

[b] Significance levels are for the monthly returns within the year and
are denoted by * at .10 level and ** at .05 level.

[c]
CHL — Channel	LSO — L-S-O Price Channel
PAR — Parabolic	REF — Reference Deviation
DRM — Directional Movement	DMC — Dual Moving Average Crossover
RNQ — Range Quotient	DRI — Directional Indicator
DRP — Directional Parabolic	MAB — Moving Average w/% Price Band
MII — MII Price Channel	ALX — Alexander's Filter Rule

Table 7. Annual Mean Returns by Commodity for All Twelve Systems, 1978-1984.[a]

Contract	CHL	PAR	DRM	RNQ	DRP	MII	LSO	REF	DMC	DRI	MAB	ALX	Average Return
						(%)							
Corn	22.4*	3.8	29.8**	-6.2	30.1**	43.3**	10.7	4.6	37.9**	-2.9	-4.7	22.9	16.0
Cocoa	10.0	-101.7	-121.9	-345.0	-112.1	-73.6	-256.9	-120.5	-72.9	-281.8	-219.2	-35.2	-144.2
Copper	-15.4	2.9	-46.1	-78.4	-4.2	-31.4	-83.0	-66.2	-39.8	-94.3	-118.4	-16.8	-49.3
L. Cattle	-12.2	-28.4	-12.4	-72.5	-16.5	-34.8	-44.9	-56.3	-11.4	-70.0	-58.9	-5.5	-35.3
P. Bellies	-30.8	22.0	-6.8	-134.4	4.8	20.6	-117.4	-145.3	-6.5	-127.6	-112.0	-12.1	-53.8
Lumber	38.7*	-43.6	-.4	-19.2	-40.6	31.3	-46.3	-18.4	36.6**	-19.1	-47.1	24.6	-8.6
Soybeans	7.7	-19.1	25.8*	-57.9	-10.0	13.3	-21.5	-45.8	2.6	-10.7	-22.5	13.1	-10.4
Silver	60.5**	54.4	.2	-15.9	82.3*	-19.1	12.5	-72.4	34.2*	-76.2	-18.0	55.9	8.2
Sugar	103.4**	46.2	61.2*	-42.1	63.4	72.6**	-.8	-47.3	82.3**	17.6	15.2	71.6**	36.9
B. Pound	-3.5	8.1	20.7**	-36.1	30.3	1.9	-7.8	3.5	25.9	-10.2	-65.8	-39.8	-6.1
Deutschmark	66.5**	35.4*	68.2**	18.8	78.0**	63.3**	19.2	-17.8	46.3**	24.6	6.6	-50.0	29.9
T. Bills	108.7	48.5	132.7	-40.1	225.5**	189.9	221.8	239.8	127.8	39.2	-12.0	32.9	109.6

[a] Calculation of annual percent returns assumes the total investment is the 30% initial investment in margins plus the 70% held back for potential margin calls. Margins vary by commodity but are assumed to be about 10% of contract value. For example, a trader who invested $1000 would use $300 for initial margins and $700 for potential margin calls. If profits were $100 over the period, then the percent return would be 10%.

[b] CHL = Channel   LSO = L-S-O Price Channel   MII = MII Price Channel

PAR = Parabolic   REF = Reference Deviation   DRP = Directional Parabolic

DRM = Directional Movement   RNQ = Range Quotient   DRI = Directional Indicator

DMC = Dual Moving Average Crossover   MAB = Moving Average w/% Price Band   ALX = Alexander's Filter Rule

One asterisk means the mean return is significant at the 10 percent level and two asterisks means it is significant at the 5 percent level.

generated significant returns while significant returns to silver were possible in 1979, 1980, 1982, and 1984. Significant profits to sugar occurred in 1980, 1981, and 1984 with Treasury Bills generating significant profits every year except 1981 and 1983. The British pound had significant returns every year except 1983 and 1984, and the Deutsche Mark generated significant returns in every year except 1983. All the above suggests that significant profits are very dependent on the market, trading system and time frame. Furthermore, four out of the twelve commodities generated significant positive returns in 1984, thus positive returns to technical analysis are still evident.

Irwin and Brorsen (1984) suggested that profits from trading systems may have decreased in 1982 and 1983 because of an "explosion" in the private use of technical analysis enhanced by the microcomputer. This is generally supported by the results of this study and actual futures fund returns (Irwin and Brorsen, 1985). However, other results, specifically the CHL results from this study and individual commodity returns by year, suggest that possible profits may still be attainable but the key is the portfolio of commodities used to generate the returns. This points out that efficiency is a market level concept. A portfolio test may be a more powerful test of market efficiency, but it is the individual markets which are inefficient, not all futures markets. Future research is needed to develop ways of identifying when a market is likely to be inefficient so that trading can be concentrated in these markets.

Since significant positive profits have been found, disequilibrium pricing models seem to be a better description of short run commodity price movements. Disequilibrium pricing models suggest trends are possible as markets adjust to information shocks. The adjustment period to a new equilibrium is slowed by transaction costs and the cost of acquiring and evaluating information.

Price adjustments are not instantaneous. As the market encounters "friction" while it moves to a new state of equilibrium, a trend develops. Therefore, the trading system picks up on this trend and generates profits. This would suggest trends and trading profits may be a natural occurrence of the market. These general findings are consistent with Taylor (1985) who argued that empirical results for several futures markets support the conclusion that a small amount of relevant information is reflected slowly by prices, thus causing price trends. However positive returns alone may not be sufficient to refute weak form efficiency. The results of an alternative market efficiency test are presented next.

Jensen Test of Market Efficiency

Testing weak form efficiency using a zero return benchmark has been criticized by Danthine and Panton. They have suggested that to test weak form efficiency, an efficient market should be defined as a market that does not yield a profit above a return to risk. Jensen's test of market efficiency uses the capital asset pricing model framework to account for risk in the returns from the trading systems.

Table 8 presents the results of the Jensen test of weak form efficiency. Again the same four systems--the channel (CHL), directional
parabolic (DRP), MII price channel (MII) and the dual moving average
crossover (DMC)--have significant intercepts and thus significant above
normal returns. Significance is at least at the 10 percent level. Furthermore all twelve of the system's coefficients (beta coefficients) on
the S&P 500 returns are negative. This is consistent with Irwin and
Brorsen's (1985) findings with respect to futures funds returns and the
S&P 500. Seven of the twelve are significantly negative at the 10 percent level. This would suggest futures market returns from these systems are negatively correlated with stock market returns. However, all
the R^2's for the regression equations are very low, indicating limited
relationship between commodity portfolio returns and stock market
returns.

The implications for weak form efficiency is to suggest some of
these futures markets were weak form inefficient from 1978 through 1984.
One-third of the trading systems produced returns significantly above
the market line for the period. Therefore this set of conclusions only
enhances the previous ones. The hypothesis that no trading system can
generate a return above a return to risk is rejected. In summation the
capability of using past prices to generate profits above a return to
risk appears evident and futures market inefficiency is present.

Preferred System(s)

Simulating twelve trading system returns provided for the possibility of looking at the preferred system(s). These procedures took two
forms, (1) using Modern Portfolio Theory based on earlier work by
Markowitz's E-V frontier and (2) Stochastic Dominance procedures developed by Meyer. The Markowitz (E-V) results will be presented first,
followed by the stochastic dominance results and a summary.

E-V Simulation

Table 9 shows the efficient set of risk and expected returns which
could be obtained from a portfolio of trading systems. Risk is measured
as monthly standard deviation and is expressed in percent. At lower
levels of risk (10.0, 10.1) most of a trader's assets would be in the
parabolic (PAR) and dual moving average crossover (DMC), while obtaining
a return of .5 to 1.0 percent a month. However as risk is increased
beyond 10.1 percent, a steady amount of the trader's assets would flow
to the channel (CHL) system, with expected return increasing rapidly.
At a risk level of 12.3 percent, 77% of a trader's assets would be in
the CHL system with an expected return of 2.7 percent a month. This
would indicate that at higher levels of risk and return, the CHL system
becomes the more efficient system in that it generates the higher return
given the level of risk (Markowitz efficient).

The risk reduction potential through diversification is not large.
A trader would have to accept an 81% (2.7 to .5) reduction in returns to
gain 20% reduction in risk (12.3 to 10.0), thus the benefits of risk

Table 8. Regression Coefficients for Tests of Excess Returns Based on the Capital Asset Pricing Model, 1978-1984.

Trading System[a]	Independent Variable				
	Intercept		S&P 500 Returns		
	Coefficient[b]	t-value	Coefficient[b]	t-value	R^2
CHL	2.9766***	2.145	-.5312*	-1.669	.0329
PAR	.5231	.414	-.6131***	-2.117	.0518
DRM	1.1677	.827	-.2815	-.870	.0091
RNQ	-6.4410	-3.718	-.4432	-1.116	.0150
DRP	2.9707**	1.727	-.8467***	-2.147	.0532
MII	2.3456**	1.735	-.6687***	-2.157	.0537
LSO	-2.4210	-1.613	-.5184*	-1.506	.0269
REF	-2.2610	-1.173	-.2952	-.668	.0054
DMC	1.9634*	1.369	-.1954	-.594	.0043
DRI	-4.4566	-2.378	-.5553	-1.292	.0200
MAB	-4.7803	-3.046	-.6999**	-1.945	.0441
ALX	1.2515	.880	-.4701*	-1.442	.0247

[a] CHL — Channel   LSO — L-S-O Price Channel

   PAR — Parabolic   REF — Reference Deviation

   DRM — Directional Movement   DMC — Dual Moving Average Crossover

   RNQ — Range Quotient   DRI — Directional Indicator

   DRP — Directional Parabolic   MAB — Moving Average w/% Price Band

   MII — MII Price Channel   ALX — Alexander's Filter Rule

[b] Significance levels using a one-tailed test are denoted by: * at 10 percent level, ** at 5 percent level, and *** at 2.5 percent level.

Table 9. Efficient Risk-Return Tradeoff Curve for Portfolios of All Twelve Trading Systems.

Expected Return[a]	Standard Deviation[a]	Portfolio Proportions											
		CHL	PAR	DRM	RNQ	DRP	MII	LSO	REF	DMC	DRI	MAB	ALX
(%)	(%)												
.5	10.0	.02	.44	.00	.00	.00	.02	.13	.00	.25	.00	.00	.14
1.0	10.1	.06	.41	.00	.00	.00	.08	.04	.00	.25	.00	.00	.16
1.5	10.3	.20	.30	.00	.00	.00	.14	.00	.00	.21	.00	.00	.15
2.0	10.9	.42	.13	.00	.00	.00	.19	.00	.00	.14	.00	.00	.12
2.5	11.8	.60	.00	.00	.00	.10	.18	.00	.00	.08	.00	.00	.04
2.7	12.3	.77	.00	.00	.00	.14	.09	.00	.00	.00	.00	.00	.00
2.8	12.8	1.00	.00	.00	.00	.00	.00	.00	.00	.00	.00	.00	.00

[a] Monthly.

[b]
CHL = Channel

PAR = Parabolic

DRM = Directional Movement

DMC = Dual Moving Average Crossover

LSO = L-S-O Price Channel

REF = Reference Deviation

RNQ = Range Quotient

MAB = Moving Average w/% Price Band

MII = MII Price Channel

DRP = Directional Parabolic

DRI = Directional Indicator

ALX = Alexander's Filter Rule

reduction through diversification may not outweigh the cost of reducing return (and costs associated with trading multiple systems). Therefore, using the channel only may be preferred rather than using multiple systems. The small gain to diversification across systems is directly related to the high correlations among the returns (Table 10). Note that even though the directional parabolic (DRP) had a high mean monthly return (Table 4) it still does not significantly contribute to the efficient solution even at high levels of expected return. This is because it is much more risky than the CHL system, thus a trader who is risk averse and wants to maximize his return for a given risk level would put most of his assets in the CHL system, not the DRP, even though both have large significant monthly returns.

Stochastic Dominance Procedure

The stochastic dominance procedure ranks distributions based on the level of risk aversion. This procedure can determine a preferred trading system based on risk and return. Table 11 presents the efficient distributions. Negative values of $r(x)$ represent risk-seeking behavior. A risk seeking trader should use the DRP system. If a trader is risk neutral he would be indifferent to the CHL or DRP. Finally, a risk averse trader (both $r(X)$'s positive) would use the CHL system exclusively.

The results of the stochastic dominance tests are consistent with the E-V simulation. If an investor is risk averse, the CHL system is the dominant system and most, if not all, of a traders funds would be invested in that system. Furthermore, the CHL also generates the largest expected return while at the same time being an efficient risk averse system.

Given the superiority of the CNL system from the above conclusions, it could be argued that the CNL offers a more powerful test of market efficiency than the present benchmark system for academic studies, which is Alexander's filter rule (ALX). Therefore substituting the CNL for the ALX in empirical work is suggested.

SUMMARY AND CONCLUSIONS

Trading of twelve technical systems was simulated in order to study weak form market efficiency and determine the preferred trading system(s) based on risk and return. Market efficiency is important to researchers who want to know whether the Martingale model or disequilibrium pricing models are a better description of short-run futures price movements. Furthermore, market efficiency is important to users of futures markets who base their current and future decisions on the price signals from the market, thus poor price signals could lead to poor decisions. Finally, the preferred trading system(s) is important to traders who use technical trading systems.

Trading of the twelve technical systems was simulated for a diversified portfolio of twelve commodities from 1978 through 1984. The

Table 10. Correlations of Aggregate Monthly Returns from All Twelve

Trading Systems.

Trading System[a,b]

System	CHL	PAR	DRM	RNQ	DRP	MII	LSO	REF	DMC	DRI	MAB
PAR	.57										
DRM	.72	.61									
RNQ	.70	.41	.70								
DRP	.65	.81	.79	.57							
MII	.75	.54	.67	.73	.67						
LSO	.59	.43	.53	.68	.54	.70					
REF	.55	.37	.57	.66	.52	.54	.60				
DMC	.72	.41	.68	.78	.55	.74	.58	.57			
DRI	.71	.42	.69	.77	.55	.70	.59	.66	.64		
MAB	.72	.55	.75	.74	.69	.69	.63	.60	.78	.72	
ALX	.58	.55	.62	.55	.57	.57	.58	.51	.52	.56	.57

[a] CHL - Channel   LSO - L-S-O Price Channel

PAR - Parabolic   REF - Reference Deviation

DRM - Directional Movement   DMC - Dual Moving Average Crossover

RNQ - Range Quotient   DRI - Directional Indicator

DRP - Directional Parabolic   MAB - Moving Average w/% Price Band

MII - MII Price Channel   ALX - Alexander's Filter Rule

[b] All coefficients significant at the .01 percent level with the exception
of REF and PAR coefficient which is significant at the .05 percent level.

Table 11. Stochastic Dominance Comparisons of All Twelve Monthly Return

Distributions from the Twelve Trading Systems, 1978-1984.[a]

$r_1(X)$	$r_2(X)$	Efficient Distribution(s)
-.10	-.08	Directional Parabolic
-.08	-.06	Direational Parabolic
-.06	-.04	Directional Parabolic
-.04	-.02	Directional Parabolic
-.02	-.005	Directional Parabolic
-.005	.005	Channel and Directional Parabolic
.005	.02	Channel
.02	.04	Channel
.04	.06	Channel
.06	.08	Channel
.08	.10	Channel

[a] Negative values of r(x) represent risk seeking preferences while positive values represent risk aversion. Risk neutrality is represented by the interval [-.005, .005].

trading systems consisted of channel systems--close channel, MII price channel, L-S-O price channel; momentum oscillators-directional indicator, directional movement, range quotient, reference deviation; moving averages-moving average with percentage price band, dual moving average crossover; a combination system-directional parabolic; and systems with trailing stops-parabolic time/price, Alexander's filter rule. The commodities were corn, cocoa, copper, live cattle, pork bellies, lumber, soybeans, silver, sugar, Treasury Bills, British Pound, and Deutsche Mark. All returns were based on optimized parameters traded after the optimization period. Returns were calculated, assuming a $100 per trade commission cost. The systems were compared considering risk and return.

The Martingale model suggests trading returns cannot be above zero, while the Efficient Market Hypothesis suggests trading returns cannot be above a return to risk. These two models suggest two testable hypotheses: 1) the trading systems cannot generate a return above zero and 2) if positive profits are found, they would not be above a return for risk. Additionally the presence of profits could suggest alternate models to describe futures prices. Disequilibrium pricing models were suggested as an alternative to the Martingale model, because they allowed for positive returns. Therefore trading system tests of market efficiency are very important to not only users of the market, but also for researchers trying to model futures prices.

Four of twelve trading systems generated aggregate portfolio returns significantly greater than zero. These systems were the channel, directional parabolic, MII price channel, and the dual moving average crossover. Since positive profits were found the Martingale Efficient Markets Model did not represent futures price movements from 1978 through 1984.

Additionally significant profits were found at the market level with respect to at least one trading system in eight out of twelve commodities during the period. These commodities were corn, lumber, soybeans, silver, sugar, British Pound, Deutsche Mark and Treasury Bills. The commodities exhibiting the highest number of significant returns were the Deutsche Mark, sugar, and corn. The markets had large profits in different years over the study, but generally profits decreased in the 1983 and 1984 period. This could be attributed to increased use of the systems making markets more efficient, thus profits harder to obtain. Another possibility is that macroeconomic factors have changed (e.g., less inflation), and thus markets have been subjected to fewer large information shocks.

This last suggestion of markets being subjected to information shocks has implications for disequilibrium pricing models. Disequilibrium pricing models suggest commodity price trends are possible as markets adjust to information shocks. The adjustment period to a new equilibrium is slowed by factors such as transaction costs and the cost of acquiring and evaluating information. This suggests that as futures markets react to large information shocks the market encounters friction as it moves to a new equilibrium resulting in trends which produce profits to a trend-following trading system. The results of this study are consistent with this logic, and thus disequilibrium pricing models were considered the better model to describe the price movements of futures markets during the period 1978 through 1984.

A final market efficiency test using trading systems involved testing whether the returns from technical analysis were above a return to risk. The results of this test also indicated that U.S. futures markets were inefficient during the simulation period, but at weaker significance levels. The same four systems--channel, directional parabolic, MII price channel, and dual moving average crossover--had monthly aggregate portfolio returns above a return to risk, thus weak form efficiency was rejected. Furthermore, since accounting for risk had little effect on the conclusions, the adjustment for risk may not be important in future research. However, these findings do enhance the results found with the Martingale Efficient Markets Test because the Jensen test is a stronger test of market efficiency since it accounts for risk.

The measures used to determine preferred trading systems or system used were an expected return-variance approach (E-V) and a stochastic dominance approach. The results of the E-V model indicated that at lower levels of risk most of a risk averse trader's assets should be in the parabolic and dual moving average crossover. As risk increases more of the trader's assets would be in the channel system. However the potential for risk reduction through diversification is not large and thus the cost of lowering the expected return may outweigh the gain from reducing risk. The results of the stochastic dominance suggested the channel was the dominant system if a trader was risk averse and only wanted to use one system. If a trader was risk seeking, the directional parabolic would be the dominant system. Both measures suggest the channel system as being the risk-return efficient system.

These results show that conclusions regarding efficiency are quite sensitive to the choice of technical trading system. The ability of the channel system to outperform other systems would suggest that the channel would provide a more powerful test of market efficiency in academic studies. The channel outperformed Alexander's filter rule which is currently the benchmark system in academic studies. Additionally, Alexander's filter rule failed to reject efficiency in this study although it did generate a positive return. Thus, substituting the channel for Alexander's filter rule is suggested in future empirical work to test market efficiency using trading systems.

REFERENCES

Alexander, Sidney S. "Price Movements in Speculative Markets: Trends or Random Walks," Industrial Management Review, 2(1961):7-26.

Arrow, K.J. Essay in Theory of Risk Bearing. Chicago: Markham, 1971.

Arrow, K. and F. Hahn. General Competitive Analysis. San Francisco: Holden Day, 1971.

Barker, David. "A Moving Average with a % Price Band," Report No. 1, Commodity Systems Reports, 1981.

_____. "The Directional Indicator," Report No. 2, Commodity Systems Reports, 1981.

_____. "L-S-O Price Channel," Report No. 3, Commodity Systems Reports, 1981.

_____. "The Range Quotient System," Report No. 4, Commodity Systems Reports, 1981.

_____. "M-II Price Channel System," Report No. 5, Commodity Systems Reports, 1981.

_____. "The Dual Moving Average Crossover System, Report No. 6, Commodity Systems Reports, 1981.

_____. "The Outside Price Channel System," Report No. 7, Commodity Systems Reports, 1981.

_____. "The Outside Price Channel System," Report No. 8, Commodity Systems Reports, 1981.

Baxter, Jennifer, Thomas E. Conine, Jr., and Maurry Tamarkin. "On Commodity Market Risk Premiums: Additional Evidence," The Journal of Futures Markets, 5(1985):11-125.

Bellemore, D.H., H.E. Phillips, and J.C. Ritchie. Investment Analysis and Portfolio Selection: An Integrated Approach. Cincinnati: South-Western Publishing Co., 1979.

Beja, A. and M.B. Goldman. "On the Dynamic Behavior of Prices in Disequilibrium," Journal of Finance, 34(1980):235-247.

Black, S.W. "Rational Response to Shocks in a Dynamic Model of Capital Asset Prices," American Economic Review, 66(1976):767-779.

Brorsen, B.W. and S. Irwin. "Evaluation of Commodity Funds," Review of Research in Futures Markets, 4(1985):84-94.

_____. "Has the Growth of Commodity Pools Affected Price Volatility?," Paper presented at NCR-134 Conference, April 23, 1986.

Carter, C.A., G.C. Rausser, and A. Schmitz. "Efficient Asset Portfolios and the Theory of Normal Backwardization," Journal of Political Economy, 91(1983):319-331.

Dale, C. and R. Workaman. "Patterns of Price Movement in Treasury Bill Futures," Journal of Economics and Business, 33(1981):81-87.

Danthine, J.P. "Martingale Market Efficiency and Commodity Prices," European Economic Review, 10(1977):1-17.

Donchian, R.D. "Trends Following Methods in Commodity Analysis," Commodity Year Book - 1957, Commodity Research, Inc., 1957, pp. 35-47.

Dunn, D. "Personal Conversations," West Lafayette, IN. January-December, 1985.

Dunn & Hargitt, Inc. "The Dunn & Hargitt Commodity Data Bank," West Lafayette, IN.

Dusak, K. "Futures Trading and Investor Returns: An Investigation of Commodity Market Risk Premiums," Journal of Political Economy, 81(1973):1387-1406.

Fama, E.F. "Efficient Capital Markets: A Review of Theory and Empirical Work," Journal of Business, 25(1970):383-417.

Fama, E.F. and M.E. Blume. "Filter Rules and Stock Market Trading," Journal of Business, 39(1966):226-241.

Gardner, B. "Commentary," Review of Research in Futures Markets, 1(1982):105-108.

Grossman, S.J. and J.E. Stiglitz. "On the Impossibility of Informationally Efficient Markets," American Economic Review, 70(1980):393-408.

Hieronymus, T.A. Economics of Futures Trading. Commodity Research Bureau, Inc., 1971.

Houthakker, H. "Systematic and Random Elements in Short-Term Price Movements," American Economic Review51(1961):164-1722.

Ibbotson Associates. Stocks, Bonds, Bills, and Inflation: 1985 Yearbook, Chicago: Capital Market Research Center, 1985.

Institute for Technical Trading Research and Education, Inc. New Concepts - A Computer Takes A Look at New Concepts in Technical Trading Systems, 1980.

Irwin, S.H. and B.W. Brorsen. "An Economic Evaluation of Technical Analysis," Staff Paper No. 84-7, Department of Agricultural Economics, Purdue Un @e sity, June 1984.

_____. "Public Futures Funds," Journal of Futures Markets, 5(Summer 1985):149-172.

Irwin, S.H. and J.W. Uhrig. "Statistical and Trading System Analysis of Weak Form Efficiency in U.S. Futures Markets," Agricultural Experiment Station Bulletin No. 421, Department of Agricultural Economics, Purdue University, 1983.

Jensen, M.L. "The Performance of Mutual Funds in the Period 1945-64," Journal of Finance, 23(1968):389-416.

_____. "Some Anomalous Evidence Regarding Marketing Efficiency: An Editorial Introduction," Journal of Financial Economics, 9(1978):95-101.

Kaufman, P.J. Technical Analysis in Commodities, Toronto: Ronald Press, 1980.

King, R.P. and L.J. Robison. "An Interval Approach to Measuring Decision Makers Preference," American Journal of Agricultural Economics, 63(1981):510-520.

Kramer, R.A. and R.D. Pope. "Participation in Farm Commodity Programs: A Stochastic Dominance Analysis," American Journal of Agricultural Economics, 63(1981):119-128.

Laing, Jonathan R. "200 Million Swinger," Barron's, February 17, 1986, pp. 8-9, 35-36, 38.

Leroy, S.P. "Risk Aversion and the Martingale Property of Prices," International Economic Review, 14(1973):436-446.

Leuthold, R.M. "Random Walk and Price Trends: The Live Cattle Futures Market," Journal of Finance, 27(1972):;879-889.

Lukac, Louis P. "Similarities of Technical Trading Systems and Market Efficiency Implications," M.S. Thesis, Department of Agricultural Economics, Purdue University, 1985.

Mandlebrot, B. "Forecasts of Futures Prices, Unbiased Markets, and Martingale Models," Journal of Business, 39(1966):242-255.

Markowitz, H. Portfolio Selection: Efficient Diversification of Investment. New York: John Wiley and Sons, 1959.

Martell, T.F. and G.C. Phillipatos. "Adaption, Information, and Dependence in Commodity Markets," Journal of Finance, 29(1974):493-498.

Meyer, J. "Choice Among Distributions," Journal of Economic Theory, 14(1977):327-336.

Nawrocki, D. "Adaptive Trading Rules and Dynamic Market Disequilibrium," Applied Economics, 16(1984):1-14.

Panton, D.B. "A Semi-Strong Form Evaluation of the Efficiency of the Hog Futures Market: Comment," American Journal of Agricultural Economics, 62(1980):584.

Peterson, P.E. and R.M. Leuthold. "Using Mechanical Trading Systems to Evaluate the Weak Form Efficiency of Futures Markets," Southern Journal of Agricultural Economics, 14(1982):147-152.

Praetz, P.D. "On the Methodology of Testing for Independence in Futures Prices: Comment." With Replies by Robert M. Bear and Richard A. Stevenson and Raymond M. Leuthold. Journal of Finance, 31(1976):977-985.

Pratt, J.W. "Risk Aversion in the Small and Large," Econometrica, 32(1964):122-136.

Samuelson, P.A. "Proof That Properly Anticipated Prices Fluctuate Randomly," Industrial Management Review, 6(1965):41-50.

Shannon, Robert E. System Simulation: The Art and Science. Englewood Cliffs, NJ: Prentice Hall, 1975.

Sharpe, W.F. "Capital Asset Prices: A Theory of Market Equilibrium Under Conditions of Risk," Journal of Finance, 19(1964):425-442.

Smidt, S. "A Test of Serial Independence of Price Changes in Soybean Futures," Food Research Institute Studies, 5(1965):117-136.

Stevenson, R.A. and R.M. Bear. "Commodity Futures, Trends, or Random Walks," Journal of Finance, 25(1970):65-81.

Taylor, S.J. "The Behaviour of Futures Prices Over Time," Applied Economics, 17(1985):713-734.

Wilder, J.W., Jr. New Concepts in Technical Trading Systems. Trend Research, Greensboro, NC: Hunter Publishing Company, 1978.

Appendix A

The Close Channel System (CHL)

The Close Channel System or Channel is a member of the price channel family of technical systems. This system is very similar to the Donchian System introduced in 1960 (Donchian), with the only difference between the two being that the Close Channel uses days to set the price channel and the Donchian uses weeks, thus the Donchian is considered a subset of the Close Channel. The Close Channel generates a buy signal anytime the current futures price is outside (higher than) the highest price in a specified time interval and generates a sell signal anytime the current futures price breaks outside (lower than) the lowest price in the same interval. This system is always in the market in that it always generates a signal for the trader to take a position, long or short, in the futures market. Dunn suggests this system or a form of it is widely used by traders.

Specifications of Close Channel:

A. Definitions and Abbreviations for Close Channel

   1. A price channel is a time interval (present day included) which is L days in length.

   2. The highest high is the highest price in the previous (L-1) days.

   3. The lowest low is the lowest price in the previous (L-1) days.

   4. Offset and reverse (OAR) is a term describing the offsetting of a previous futures position and the initiating of a new position which is opposite of the previous one.

B. Trading Rules for Close Channel

   1. Buy long when today's high or open is above the highest high in daily price channel.

   2. Sell short when today's low or open is below the lowest low in the daily price channel.

   3. Entry or exit of a position occurs if (a) the open is above (below) the daily channel high (low) on a random day then a long (short) position is entered (exited) at the open price, (b) if the daily high (low) is above (below) the channel high (low) then a buy (sell) signal is given, with the entry (exit) price assumed to be just above (below) the channel high (low).

   4. System is always in the market -- never goes neutral.

C. Parameter for Close Channel

1. L-number of days in price channel.

L-S-O Price Channel (LSO)

The L-S-O Price Channel belongs to the price channel group of technical trading systems. It differentiates itself in that the system can
be either long, short, or out of the market (L-S-O). A fundamental
characteristic of all price channels is the comparison of today's price
level with price levels some specified number of days in the past. The
L-S-O Price Channel, introduced by Barker in May of 1981, uses today's
close and compares it with the price action of an interval of days near
the end of the channel. An important point is that the system is not
always in the market and thus it can go neutral for a period of time.

Specifications of L-S-O Price Channel:

A. Definitions and Abbreviations for L-S-O Price Channel

1. N — number of days in the price channel including today's
price.

2. L — number of consecutive days in the reference interval
(defined below).

3. The Reference Interval (RI) is the group of consecutive
days at the opposite end of the price channel from today's
price, L days in length.

4. The highest high in the reference interval is defined as
the Reference Interval High (RIH).

5. The lowest low in the reference interval is defined as the
Reference Interval Low (RIL).

6. The exit point to go neutral, known as a stop, is defined
as (RIH + RIL). This applies if the system is long or
short.

B. Trading Rules for L-S-O Price Channel

1. Buy long, on the close, if today's close is higher
(greater) than the reference interval high within the N-day
channel.

2. Sell short, on the close, if today's close is lower (less)
than the reference interval low within the N-day channel.

3. If long (short), place a sell (buy) stop order halfway
between the RIH and RIL; (RIJ + RIL). This is an intraday
stop calculated everyday.

4. If the stop is triggered the system is stopped out and the trader has a neutral position.

C. Parameters for L-S-O Price Channel

1. N, the number of days in price channel, today inclusive.

2. L, the number of days in the Reference Interval.

MII Price Channel System (MII)

The MII Price Channel is a price channel type technical trading system which is always in the market. Long or short positions are established and maintained on the basis of comparing today's close with the first day of the price channel. This system is different from the close channel because it uses the first day of the price channel as a reference to trigger a trade. The MII Price Channel generates a buy signal when today's close is above both the high of day 1 of the price channel and yesterday's high and generates a sell when today's close is below both the low of the first day of the price channel and yesterday's low. This system always generates a buy or sell signal for the trader to take a position in the futures market and was introduced by Barker in July of 1981.

Specifications of the MII Price Channel:

A. Definitions and Abbreviations for MII Price Channel

1. The Price Channel is N consecutive days of futures prices including today.

2. The Reference Day (RD) is the first day of the price channel.

3. The Reference Day Theoretical High (RDTH) is the high of the RD (1st day) or the previous day's close, whichever is higher.

4. The Reference Day Theoretical Low (RDTL) is the low of the RD (1st day) or the previous day's close, whichever is lower.

5. Stop Close Only (SCO) is the order used to trigger a reverse in position.

6. Offset and Reverse (OAR) describes the liquidating of a current position and the simultaneous establishment of an opposite position.

B. Trading Rules for MII Price Channel

1. Buy long if today's close is greater (above) the RDTH. Initiate a SCO order.

2. Sell short if today's close is less (below) the RDTL. Initiate a SCO order.

3. After the initial position is taken, the system offsets and reverses (OAR).

C. Parameter for MII Price Channel

1. N, the length of the price channel.

The Directional Indicator System (DRI)

The Directional Indicator belongs to a group of technical trading systems known as momentum oscillators. They derive their name from the fact that buy, sell, and exit signals are obtained from numbers which oscillate above and below a neutral point, usually a zero value (Barker). The rationale behind momentum oscillators is to try to detect trends through the magnitude of futures price changes, opposed to the absolute level of futures prices on which the channel systems are based. The Directional Indicator estimates a trend by determining the variability in the market and assigning a numerical value to it. This measure is used to determine significant excess of either up or down movement, and thus indicates market momentum or direction. Oscillators are used widely, but usually in conjunction with other system(s) rather than the sole trading indicator. Barker formally published the Directional Indicator in April of 1981. The system produces trading signals based on entry levels, which when crossed by the DI (explained below) produces a signal. This system can go neutral.

Specifications of the Directional Indicator:

A. Definitions and Abbreviations of the Directional Indicator

1. The Net Price Change (NPC) is defined as today's close minus the closing price N days ago.

2. The Total Price Change (TPC) is defined as the sum of the absolute value of all daily price changes (closing price to closing price) over N days.

3. The Directional Indicator (DI), expressed as a percent, is defined as the (NPC + TPC) x 100.

4. The Entry Threshold (ET) is the percent (positive or negative) which when crossed by the DI generates a buy or sell signal.

5. Neutral Zone (NZ) is the DI values between the positive and negative ET's.

B. Trading Rules for the Directional Indicator

1. Buy long on tomorrow's open when today's DI becomes equal to or more positive than the positive entry threshold (+ET).

2. Sell (offset) on tomorrow's open when today's DI becomes less than or equal to zero.

3. Sell short on tomorrow's open when today's DI becomes equal to or more negative than the negative entry threshold (-ET).

4. Buy (offset) on tomorrow's open, when today's DI becomes greater than or equal to zero.

C. Parameters for Directional Indicator

1. N, the number of days to be used to calculate the DI.

2. ET, the entry threshold (+ and -) to trigger trading.

The Directional Movement System (DRM)

The Directional Movement system is a member of the price oscillator family of technical trading systems. Wilder introduced this system in 1978. This system rates the directional movement of futures prices on a scale of zero to one hundred by the use of two market directional indicators, one positive and one negative. The true directional movement is the difference between the two indicators, thus the more (less) directional the movement of a commodity price, the greater (smaller) will be the difference between the indicators. Buy signals are generated when the positive directional indicator crosses above the negative directional indicator and sell signals are generated when the negative directional indicator crosses above the positive directional indicator. The system always generates a signal for the trader to buy or sell.

Specifications of the Directional Movement System:

A. Definitions and Abbreviations for the Directional Movement

1. N is number of days to calculate the trend or movement.

2. Positive Diqectional Movement (PDM) is the high today mjnus the high yesterday if today's high is above yesterday's, otherwise it is zero.

3. Negative Directional Movement (NDM) is the low today minus the low yesterday if today's low is below yesterday's low, otherwise it is zero.

4. In the event of an inside day (the high today is lower than the previous day's high and the low today is higher than the previous day's low) or an equal day (no change from previous day's high and low) then directional movement is zero.

5. In the event of an outside day (the high today is higher than the previous day's high and the low today is lower than the previous day's low) the directional movement is the larger of the PDM and NDM.

6. True Range (TR) which is always considered to be positive, is defined as the largest of the following:

   i) The distance between today's high and today's low.

   ii) The distance between today's high and yesterday's close.

   iii) The distance between today's low and yesterday's close.

7. The Positive Directional Indicator $(PDI)_N$ is defined as PDM_N/TR_N where N designates the summation over N days.

8. The Negative Directional Indicator $(NDI)_N$ is defined as NDM_N/TR_N where N designates the summation over N days.

9. The Extreme Point Rule (EPR) states that when the PDI_N and NDI_N cross, use the extreme point made that day as the reverse point; i.e., the high if short, the low if long.

B. Trading Rules for the Directional Movement

1. Buy long when the PDI_N crosses above the NDI_N.

2. Sell short when the NDI_N crosses below the PDI_N.

3. When long, the reverse point is the extreme point, i.e., the low made on the day of crossing.

4. When short, the reverse point is the extreme point, i.e., the high made on the day of crossing.

5. In the case of 3 and 4 above, stay with these reversals even if not reversed and even if the indexes stay crossed contrary to your position for several days. The reversal point must be crossed before offsetting and reversing.

C. Parameter for Directional Movement

    1. N, the number of days to calculate indices.

The Range Quotient System (RNQ)

This system is also a member of the momentum oscillator class of technical trading systems. It was introduced formally by Barker in June 1981. The Range Quotient System converts ranges of futures prices into a single index. It is based upon the relationship between an average daily price range and total price range over some time interval similar to other oscillators. The system does not always generate a buy or a sell signal for the trader to take a position in the futures market, thus it can go neutral.

Specifications of Range Quotient System:

A. Definitions and Abbreviations of Ranfe Quotient

    1. The True High (TH) is the higher of today's high or yesterday's close.

    2. The True Low (TL) is the lower of today's low or yesterday's close.

    3. The Daily Price Range (DR) is TH minus TL.

    4. The Average Daily Price Range (ADR) is the arithmetic mean of DR for N days.

    5. N is the number of days, today inclusive, used to calculate the Range Quotient.

    6. HH is the highest high in N days.

    7. LL is the lowest low in N days.

    8. The Total Price Range (TR) equals HH minus LL.

    9. The Range Quotient (RQ) equals (1-ADR/TR) * 100.

    10. Entry Threshold (ET) is the RQ value beyond which buy or sell signals occur.

    11. A (+) sign is assigned to RQ if today's close is above the close of day 1 of the N day interval and a (-) sign if it is below.

B. Trading Rules for Range Quotient

    1. Buy long, next day's open, if RQ is greater than +ET.

    2. Sell offset on next day's open when sign of RQ changes from (+) to (-).

3. Sell short, next day's open, if RQ is less than -ET.

4. Buy offset on next day's open when sign of RQ changes from (-) to (+).

C. Parameters for Range Quotient

1. N, the number of days to calculate the RQ.

2. ET, the value of RQ used for entry and exit rules.

The Reference Deviation System (REF)

The Reference Deviation is an oscillator type technical trading system. Barker introduced it in October 1981. This system is similar to other oscillators in that buy and sell signals are dependent on arbitrary threshold levels. However, this system is unique in that it uses a moving average as a reference point to calculate an index value or measure of volatility. This system can be neutral thus not indicating a signal to the trader.

Specifications of the Reference Deviation System:

A. Definitions and Abbreviations of the Reference Deviation

1. The Reference Moving Average (RMA) is the simple average of the closing prices over the last N days.

2. The Daily Reference Deviation (DRD) is the difference between each day's close and the RMA for that day. DRD will be positive (+) when the close is above the RMA and negative (-) when below the RMA.

3. The Net Deviation Value (NDV) is the sum of the DRD's for the previous N days.

4. The Total Deviation Value (TDV) is the sum of the absolute values of the DRD's for the previous N days.

5. The Reference Deviation Value (RDV) for a particular day is the ratio of the NDV/TDV x 100 on the particular day.

6. The Entry Threshold (ET) is the arbitrary value of the RDV beyond which buy and sell signals are generated.

B. Trading Rules for the Reference Deviation

1. Buy long on tomorrow's open if RDV is greater than +ET.

2. Sell offset on tomorrow's open ig RDV is less than zero.

3. Sell short on tomorrow's open if RDV is less than -ET.

4. Buy offset on tomorrow's open if RDV is greater than zero.

C. Parameters for Reference Deviation

    1. N, the number of days used to calculate RDV.

    2. ET, the value of RDV used for entry and exit rules.

The Simple Moving Average with Percentage Price Band (MAB)

This system belongs to a technical system group called moving averages. These technical systems are used extensively by brokers, money managers, advisors, many investors, and are published by several major popular chart services. These widely accepted technical systems take on several forms such as a simple standard moving average, an exponentially smoothed moving average or a linearly weighted moving average. Their effect is to smooth out price actions, thereby avoiding false signals produced by erratic, short-term price movements, and identifying the true, underlying trend (Barker). The Moving Average with Percent Price Band uses a simple moving average with a price band centered around it based on a percent of futures price. A signal is triggered whenever the closing price breaks outside the band, and an exit signal occurs when the price recrosses the moving average. The upper and lower price bands create a neutral zone in which the system is out of the market. This is to alleviate whipsawing in congested markets, a criticism of moving averages which leads to many unprofitable buy and sell signals being generated.

Specifications of the Simple Moving Average with Percent Price Band:

A. Trading Rules for Moving Average with Percent Price Band

    1. Buy long on tomorrow's open when today's closing price is higher than the upper band limit.

    2. Sell offset on tomorrow's open when today's closing price drops below the moving average.

    3. Sell short on tomorrow's open when today's closing price is below the lower band limit.

    4. Buy offset on tomorrow's open when today's closing price rises above the moving average.

B. Parameters of Moving Average with Percent Price Band

    1. N, the number of days to calculate the moving average.

    2. P, the percentage price band around the moving average.

Dual Moving Average Crossover System (DMC)

The dual moving average crossover system is a moving average type technical system which uses a short term moving average and a long term moving average. As the short term average moves above the longer term average an uptrend is suspected and a buy signal is given. A sell signal is given if the short term moves below the long term. This is one of the more popular moving average systems. Richard Dennis argued it is the tool used by most commodity fund advisers (Laing). Richard Donchian expressed the logic behind this:

> The chief value of moving averages as helpful tools in commodity price analysis rests on the following very simple premise: No commodity can ever stage an uptrend without first showing evidence of the preponderance of buying over selling by rising above a moving average. And no commodity can stage a downtrend without first showing evidence of more selling than buying by falling below a moving average.

Specifications of the Dual Moving Average Crossover System:

A. Abbreviations and Definitions for Dual Moving Average Crossover

    1. Number of days in longer moving average is NL.

    2. Number of days in shorter moving average is NS.

    3. Shorter moving average is SMA.

    4. Longer moving average is LMA.

    5. Offset and reverse is OAR.

B. Trading Rules for the Dual Moving Average Crossover

    1. Buy long on tomorrow's open when the SMA is greater than (above) the LMA.

    2. Sell short on tomorrow's open when the SMA is less than (below) the LMA.

    3. System is reversing, always in the market either long or short, thus is OAR when it trades.

C. Parameters for Dual Moving Average Crossover

    1. NL, the number of days in longer moving average.

    2. NS, the number of days in shorter moving average.

Parabolic Time/Price System (PAR)

This system does not fit into any of the three groups of technical systems mentioned previously. It derives its name from the fact that when charted, the stops following the trend form a pattern resembling a parabola. The Parabolic Time/Price system was introduced by Wilder in 1978. This system fits best into a category of systems which have trailing stops beneath or above the trend, similar to Alexander's Filter rule (presented later). Therefore, these systems differ from previously discussed systems. A crucial difference in this system is that the stop is a function of time and price. The time function allows the stop to move in the direction of the trade (if long will move up) while the price function regulates the distance the stop moves with the trend. Specifically a linear equation specifies the stops for a trend and when the trend crosses the stop a signal is generated. The system is always in the market giving either a buy or a sell signal.

Specifications of Parabolic Time/Price System:

A. Abbreviations and Definition of Parabolic Time/Price System

1. Extreme Pont (EP) if long (short) is the current extreme high (low) price made during the present trend.

2. Acceleration Factor (AF) is the slope of the stop line. This is increased by Increment Factor (IF) each day a new high is made in an uptrend or a new low is made in a down-trend. It is reset to the starting figure every time a new trade is generated.

3. The significant point (SIP) is the lowest price reached while in a short trend or the highest price reached while in a long trend.

4. SAR is a stop and reverse point.

   a. When entering a new position on day 1, the SAR is the previous SIP, thus if entered long (short) the SIP is the lowest (highest) price reached while in the previous short (long) trade.

   b. For the second day and thereafter the SAR is computed as follows: If long (short) find the difference between the highest (lowest) price made while in the trade (EP) and the SAR for today. Multiply the difference by the AF and add (subtract) the result from the SAR today to obtain the SAR for tomorrow. Mathematically:

   If Long: $SAR_{Tomorrow} = SAR_{Today} + AF(EP_{Trade} - SAR_{Today})$

   If Short: $SAR_{Tomorrow} = SAR_{Today} - AF(EP_{Trade} - SAR_{Today})$

   c. Use IF for the beginning value of the AF and increase its value by IF whenever a new high (if long) or new low (if short) for the trade is made. If a new high or low is not made, continue to use the AF as last increased. Do not increase the AF above .20.

   d. If long (short) never move the SAR for tomorrow above (below) the previous day's low (high) or today's low (high). If the SAR is calculated to be above (below) the previous day's low (high) or today's low (high), then use the lower low (higher high) between today and the previous day as the new SAR. Make the next day's calculations based upon this SAR.

B. Trading Rules for the Parabolic

1. Buy long at the SAR if today's price moves above the SAR.

2. Sell short at the SAR if today's price moves below the SAR.

3. In the event the SAR price cannot be attained, get in at the opening price of the next day, such as if there is a limit day.

4. System always offsets and reverses.

C. Parameter for the Parabolic Time/Price System

1. IF, the increment factor.

The Directional Parabolic System (DRP)

This system is a combination system (dual system) and is the result of combining the Directional Movement System with the Parabolic System. The underlying concept is that the systems working as a pair act as a filter to screen out trades that are against the trend, yet allowing trades that are with the trend. Generally these combination systems employ a trend indicator system (Directional Movement) and a so-called "trading system" (Parabolic). This system will take the trades in accordance with the trend and skip the trades contrary to the trend. The general rules for the directional parabolic are: 1) when in a trade, the exit and/or reverse price is the stop price of the parabolic system (trading system) regardless of the position of the Directional Movement (trend indicator system) and 2) when out of a trade (neutral or skipped reversing trade) enter when both systems signal a trade in the same direction. The system does go neutral when trades are not offset, thus the reversing trade skipped. Because each underlying system has been explained previously in this section, the emphasis below will be placed on the trading rules of this combination system.

Specifications of the Directional Parabolic System:

A. Trading Rules for the Directional Parabolic System

1. If position is long and parabolic signals short, then if DM is down (up) reverse (offset) at the parabolic stop.

2. If position is short and parabolic signals long, then if DM is down (up) offset (reverse) at the parabolic stop.

3. If position is neutral and parabolic signals long (short) then if DM is up (down) enter the market long (short) at the parabolic stop.

4. If position is neutral and DM signals long (short) then if parabolic is long (short) enter the market long (short) at the high (low) on the day +DM crossed above (below) the -DM.

B. Parameters for the Directional Parabolic System

1. N, number of days to calculate the Directional Movement.

2. IF, the increment factor for the parabolic stops.

Alexander's Filter Rule (ALX)

This system was first introduced by Alexander (1961, 1964) to analyze stock market prices and was later used in many academic studies (Peterson and Leuthold; Stevenson and Bear). This system is not widely used by traders. It is similar to the parabolic in the sense it has trailing stops about the price movements which are smaller than some pre-determined amount (filter), thus trading on only the significant price changes. Basically the system generates a buy if prices rise at least X percent from a subsequent low and sell when the price drops X percent from a subsequent high. The system can be altered to use fixed dollar amount filters, but this is not how it was simulated in this study. The system was simulated with percent filters. It is always in the market.

Specifications for Alexander's Filter Rule:

A. Definitions and Abbreviations for Alexander's Filter Rule

1. The High Extreme Point (HEP) is the highest high obtained while in a long trade.

2. The Low Extreme Point (LEP) is the lowest low obtained while in a short trade.

3. The percent filter (X%) is the percent of an extreme point used to generate trades.

B. Trading Rules for Alexander's Filter Rule

1. Buy long on the close if the closing price rises X% above an LEP.

2. Sell short on the close if the closing price falls X% below an HEP.

3. System always offsets and reverses.

C. Parameter for Alexander's Filter Rule

1. X, percent filter size.

APPENDIX B

Table A.1. Optimal Parameters for the Channel System, 1978-1984.[a]

Commodity	Trading Year						
	1978	1979	1980	1981	1982	1983	1984
Corn	10	60	25	30	50	60	60
Cocoa	40	40	40	30	30	30	30
Copper	30	15	35	15	15	15	55
Live Cattle	45	5	5	5	20	35	25
Pork Bellies	35	25	20	30	10	50	20
Lumber	15	10	10	55	55	55	55
Soybeans	10	20	35	30	40	40	40
Silver	45	15	45	15	15	15	15
Sugar	15	45	35	55	55	55	55
British Pound	--	--	15	15	5	30	35
Deutch Mark	--	--	25	25	15	5	55
Treasury Bills	--	20	20	15	10	20	20

[a]The number of days (N) which yields the highest profit over the previous three years. Parameters considered ranged from 5 to 60 days in increments of 5 days.

Table A.2. Optimal Parameters for the Parabolic System, 1978-1984.[a]

Commodity	Trading Year						
	1978	1979	1980	1981	1982	1983	1984
Corn	24	19	24	16	15	15	15
Cocoa	15	15	15	21	24	14	14
Copper	14	14	14	17	17	17	15
Live Cattle	18	15	15	21	20	22	16
Pork Bellies	18	18	15	15	15	15	22
Lumber	19	19	23	23	23	24	15
Soybeans	21	14	19	19	18	20	17
Silver	15	15	24	20	21	20	14
Sugar	18	22	17	18	16	23	16
British Pound	--	--	24	14	14	14	24
Deutch Mark	--	--	22	21	20	19	20
Treasury Bills	--	14	14	14	14	21	18

[a]The increment factor (IF) percent which yields the highest profit over the previous three years. Parameters considered ranged from 14 to 24 percent in increments of 1 percent.

Table A.3. Optimal Parameters for the Directional Movement System, 1978-1984.[a]

Commodity	Trading Year						
	1978	1979	1980	1981	1982	1983	1984
Corn	3	9	24	24	18	18	9
Cocoa	18	18	18	24	6	24	9
Copper	18	6	18	6	12	15	30
Live Cattle	12	6	9	18	21	24	12
Pork Bellies	18	15	12	15	3	3	6
Lumber	3	3	3	21	21	30	30
Soybeans	6	9	24	24	24	18	21
Silver	30	15	30	3	6	6	6
Sugar	18	24	24	3	27	27	27
British Pound	--	--	30	9	9	9	9
Deutch Mark	--	--	9	9	9	9	30
Treasury Bills	--	6	3	6	6	9	15

[a]The number of days (N) which yields the highest profit over the previous three years. Parameters considered ranged from 3 to 39 days in increments of 3 days.

Table A.4. Optimal Parameters for the Range Quotient System, 1978-
           1984.[a]

Commodity	Trading Year						
	1978	1979	1980	1981	1982	1983	1984
Corn	25,80	20,80	60,55	20,80	60,70	55,70	20,80
Cocoa	60,65	40,80	25,80	30,65	20,80	55,70	40,65
Copper	25,60	60,65	20,80	20,80	20,80	20,80	60,65
Live Cattle	40,75	40,75	20,70	25,60	25,60	25,75	25,60
Pork Bellies	45,65	45,65	20,75	25,60	50,70	50,65	45,65
Lumber	40,60	40,65	60,65	60,65	60,65	55,70	60,65
Soybeans	45,80	20,75	25,60	35,75	35,75	60,65	20,75
Silver	20,60	20,60	60,65	35,65	35,65	35,65	45,60
Sugar	30,80	55,70	20,80	25,80	25,80	25,60	45,65
British Pound	--	--	60,70	50,70	60,70	60,70	60,70
Deutch Mark	--	--	20,55	20,55	20,70	45,65	40,65
Treasury Bills	--	20,80	25,80	25,60	30,75	30,65	60,65

[a]The number of days and entry threshold percents (N,ET) which yields
the highest profit over the previous three years. Parameters
considered ranged from 20 to 70 days in increments of 5 days and 55 to
80 percent in increments of 5 percent.

Table A.5. Optimal Parameters for the Directional Parabolic (Combination) System, 1978-1984.[a]

Commodity	Trading Year						
	1978	1979	1980	1981	1982	1983	1984
Corn	3,24	6,17	3,24	18,16	18,15	18,15	18,15
Cocoa	18,15	18,15	18,15	27,21	6,24	6,14	9,14
Copper	18,14	3,14	3,14	6,17	9,17	3,15	21,14
Live Cattle	3,18	3,15	18,15	18,21	18,20	18,22	12,16
Pork Bellies	18,18	15,18	6,15	21,15	3,15	3,15	6,15
Lumber	3,19	3,19	3,23	21,23	21,23	24,24	30,15
Soybeans	9,18	3,14	3,14	24,19	24,23	18,20	21,17
Silver	27,15	3,15	30,23	3,20	6,21	3,20	3,24
Sugar	15,18	6,22	21,17	30,18	30,23	30,23	27,16
British Pound	--	--	15,24	9,14	3,14	3,14	24,24
Deutch Mark	--	--	3,22	3,21	9,20	9,19	27,20
Treasury Bills	--	6,14	3,14	9,14	3,22	9,21	6,18

[a]The number of days and acceleration factor percents (N,AF) which yields the highest profit over the previous three years. Parameters considered ranged from 3 to 30 days in increments of 3 days and 14 to 24 percent in increments of 1 percent.

Table A.6. Optimal Parameters for the MII Price Channel System, 1978-
          1984.[a]

				Trading Year			
Commodity	1978	1979	1980	1981	1982	1983	1984
Corn	70	70	55	80	60	60	60
Cocoa	80	80	30	40	20	65	40
Copper	25	10	5	5	65	75	75
Live Cattle	40	5	5	5	55	20	20
Pork Bellies	55	55	15	10	10	10	10
Lumber	10	70	20	60	60	60	75
Soybeans	45	20	35	35	50	50	60
Silver	45	55	70	20	20	35	75
Sugar	25	45	80	15	25	25	45
British Pound	--	--	5	10	5	60	60
Deutch Mark	--	--	25	25	20	5	20
Treasury Bills	--	15	15	15	15	15	15

[a]The number of days (N) which yields the highest profit over the
previous three years. Parameters considered ranged from 5 to 80 days
in increments of 5 days.

Table A.7. Optimal Parameters for the L-S-O Price Channel System,
1978-1984.[a]

Commodity	Trading Year						
	1978	1979	1980	1981	1982	1983	1984
Corn	35,12	35,15	35,15	70,15	55,90	60,90	70,60
Cocoa	70,30	30,30	30,30	25,90	20,60	70,30	45,60
Copper	30,90	60,90	65,15	25,12	40,12	25,12	70,12
Live Cattle	20,15	40,60	25,30	35,15	35,15	35,15	20,60
Pork Bellies	50,60	25,30	20,30	30,60	50,30	55,12	50,90
Lumber	20,30	60,12	20,90	60,12	60,30	60,30	60,30
Soybeans	50,60	50,60	35,60	50,30	50,30	50,30	25,90
Silver	60,12	60,12	65,60	20,60	20,60	20,60	20,12
Sugar	20,30	55,12	20,12	20,30	30,60	30,60	45,30
British Pound	--	--	50,90	35,60	65,60	65,30	65,30
Deutch Mark	--	--	20,12	25,90	55,15	40,90	25,30
Treasury Bills	--	20,60	20,12	25,12	25,15	25,12	20,90

[a]The number of days in channel and reference interval (N,RI) which yields the highest profit over the previous three years. Parameters considered for N ranged from 20 to 70 days in increments of 5 days and parameters considered for RI ranged from 12 to 90 days in increments of 3 days.

Table A.8. Optimal Parameters for the Reference Deviation System, 1978-1984.[a]

Commodity	Trading Year						
	1978	1979	1980	1981	1982	1983	1984
Corn	20,10	30,80	35,70	45,10	40,10	40,10	45,20
Cocoa	50,70	50,40	50,40	50,40	20,10	20,10	20,70
Copper	20,10	50,10	45,80	15,80	25,10	10,80	50,60
Live Cattle	5,80	5,80	50,80	25,20	25,10	25,50	15,20
Pork Bellies	30,40	15,10	10,10	20,10	40,70	40,20	5,10
Lumber	50,50	40,80	50,80	45,10	45,10	35,10	35,70
Soybeans	25,10	25,10	25,10	25,10	20,20	20,20	15,10
Silver	40,30	45,10	50,20	15,30	15,10	25,40	25,40
Sugar	25,80	35,50	30,10	10,20	25,10	10,50	30,20
British Pound	--	--	50,10	25,10	25,10	20,20	20,20
Deutch Mark	--	--	10,30	10,30	40,20	15,50	50,70
Treasury Bills	--	10,10	10,10	20,50	10,20	10,20	10,20

[a]The number of days and entry threshold percent (N,ET) which yields the highest profit over the previous three years. Parameters ranged from 5 to 50 days in increments of 5 days and 10 to 80 percent in increments of 10 percent.

Table A.9. Optimal Parameters for the Dual Moving Average Crossover System, 1978-1984.[a]

Commodity	Trading Year						
	1978	1979	1980	1981	1982	1983	1984
Corn	15,40	10,35	10,45	10,65	10,65	10,65	10,60
Cocoa	20,40	15,45	25,30	15,40	20,30	15,55	20,35
Copper	10,40	10,30	10,55	25,40	25,40	10,30	25,60
Live Cattle	20,50	20,50	5,35	15,50	15,45	20,60	10,30
Pork Bellies	15,45	20,55	5,55	10,45	5,60	10,65	10,30
Lumber	25,60	20,65	20,65	20,65	25,35	25,60	25,45
Soybeans	20,50	20,45	5,45	5,60	5,60	5,60	5,35
Silver	20,65	20,65	20,65	10,30	10,50	10,50	20,50
Sugar	20,65	25,60	20,50	20,35	20,40	20,40	10,65
British Pound	--	--	5,50	5,35	20,45	20,45	20,45
Deutch Mark	--	--	5,40	5,35	5,65	10,50	10,50
Treasury Bills	--	10,30	25,60	5,35	5,35	5,35	5,45

[a]The number of days in the short moving average and longer moving average (SM,LM) which yields the highest profit over the previous three years. Parameters considered for SM ranged from 5 to 25 days in increments of 5 days and parameters considered for LM ranged from 30 to 65 days in increments of 5 days.

Table A.10. Optimal Parameters for the Directional Indicator System, 1978-1984.[a]

Commodity	Trading Year						
	1978	1979	1980	1981	1982	1983	1984
Corn	35,21	60,30	60,12	60,12	60,12	60,12	25,27
Cocoa	45,60	35,15	30,60	30,15	50,15	50,15	40,24
Copper	50,30	55,21	55,12	20,60	20,60	60,21	60,12
Live Cattle	35,60	40,30	20,60	50,27	45,15	20,24	20,90
Pork Bellies	55,30	20,90	20,90	25,30	60,24	60,24	45,30
Lumber	55,27	55,12	60,30	55,30	55,30	60,30	60,30
Soybeans	50,30	50,30	35,90	35,90	35,30	60,15	20,27
Silver	50,30	55,60	60,30	20,18	20,18	35,18	40,30
Sugar	20,30	45,27	25,30	20,24	25,18	25,12	45,27
British Pound	--	--	60,30	30,30	60,30	55,15	60,27
Deutch Mark	--	--	60,60	50,27	20,12	20,12	20,12
Treasury Bills	--	20,21	20,18	30,60	20,18	30,12	60,60

[a]The number of days and entry threshold percent (N,ET) which yields the highest profit over the previous three years. Parameters considered ranged from 20 to 60 days in increments of 5 days and 12 to 90 percent in increments of 3 percent.

Table A.11. Optimal Parameters for the Moving Average with a
Percentage Price Band System, 1978-1984.[a]

	Trading Year						
Commodity	1978	1979	1980	1981	1982	1983	1984
Corn	40,40	40,30	35,15	35,35	45,40	45,30	50,25
Cocoa	55,60	45,50	45,50	45,30	40,25	60,55	50,30
Copper	60,15	55,60	55,60	25,10	60,20	60,45	60,50
Live Cattle	10,30	50,10	45,10	35,10	35,10	35,10	35,10
Pork Bellies	55,60	60,60	20,10	30,45	15,15	5,45	5,45
Lumber	5,30	5,30	5,30	40,60	60,20	60,15	60,45
Soybeans	15,20	20,40	55,35	50,25	60,15	60,15	30,10
Silver	45,25	40,60	60,20	35,55	35,55	40,40	20,10
Sugar	45,55	60,50	45,50	15,55	40,30	50,30	55,50
British Pound	--	--	60,10	40,15	10,10	55,10	60,10
Deutch Mark	--	--	60,20	35,10	60,10	55,10	60,20
Treasury Bills	--	50,10	60,15	60,10	60,15	55,15	40,10

[a]The number of days and entry threshold percent (N,ET) which yields the
highest profit over the previous three years. Parameters considered
ranged from 5 to 60 days in increments of 5 days and 5 to 60 percent
in increments of 5 percent.

Table A.12. Optimal Parameters for the Alexander's Filter Rule System, 1978-1984.[a]

	Trading Year						
Commodity	1978	1979	1980	1981	1982	1983	1984
Corn	12	12	12	14	11	14	12
Cocoa	23	23	3	13	13	18	19
Copper	8	13	12	12	14	18	18
Live Cattle	5	5	7	7	7	3	3
Pork Bellies	10	16	12	14	6	14	10
Lumber	8	20	20	15	19	19	19
Soybeans	13	13	14	4	4	4	18
Silver	4	19	20	15	18	18	19
Sugar	24	16	16	17	17	17	23
British Pound	--	--	4	4	2	2	6
Deutch Mark	--	--	17	1	2	2	7
Treasury Bills	--	3	1	1	2	2	6

[a]The percent filter (F) which yields the highest profit over the previous three years. Parameters considered ranged from 1 to 20 percent in increments of 1 percent.

Table A.13. Optimal Parameters for All Twelve Systems, 1985.[a]

Trading System[b,c]

Contract	CHL	PAR	DRM	RNQ	DRP	MII	LSO	REF	DMC	DRI	MAB	ALX
	(N)	(IF)	(N)	(N,ET)	(N,IF)	(N)	(N,RI)	(N,ET)	(SM,LM)	(N,ET)	(N,P)	(P)
Corn	60	16	24	60,80	18,16	75	70,60	45,10	10,60	60,30	50,25	13
Cocoa	20	19	21	40,80	9,19	30	30,30	20,70	5,45	45,27	50,35	6
Copper	55	17	30	60,70	15,17	75	70,12	50,10	10,30	60,12	60,60	18
L. Cattle	25	16	12	20,80	12,16	20	20,12	30,60	15,35	20,27	35,55	15
P. Bellies	20	21	12	25,75	27,15	25	35,15	15,10	15,30	25,30	50,40	11
Lumber	55	14	30	60,65	30,14	80	70,30	30,10	25,45	60,30	60,20	18
Soybeans	50	14	6	20,55	9,14	20	20,30	15,10	5,55	20,24	25,15	11
Silver	15	14	6	35,80	3,14	10	70,30	50,30	20,65	40,15	15,20	10
Sugar	55	18	30	50,65	30,18	75	70,60	35,10	20,60	50,21	55,25	19
B. Pound	40	24	30	55,65	24,24	60	60,60	30,10	5,65	55,30	60,15	4
D. Mark	20	16	24	40,65	24,16	10	25,30	5,20	5,45	55,30	45,10	1
T. Bills	20	20	15	45,65	15,20	25	20,90	10,30	5,50	45,90	55,15	8

[a]Optimal within the ranges of the parameters tested.

[b]CHL = Channel
PAR = Parabolic
DRM = Directional Movement
RNQ = Range Quotient
DRP = Directional Parabolic
MII = MII Price Channel

LSO = L-S-O Price Channel
REF = Reference Deviation
DMC = Dual Moving Average Crossover
DRI = Directional Indicator
MAB = Moving Average w/% Price Band
ALX = Alexander's Filter Rule

[c]N = number of days; IF = (%) Increment Factor; ET = (%) Entry Threshold; RI = (Days) Reference Interval; SM = (Days) Shorter Moving Average; LM = (Days) Longer Moving Average; P = Percent.

Table A.14.   Annual Returns for Corn by Trading Year for All Twelve
Systems, 1978-1984.[a,b]

Trading System[c]	Trading Year						
	1978	1979	1980	1981	1982	1983	1984
	(%)						
CHL	-25.68	.36	23.88	58.08	25.92	61.56	16.68
PAR	-7.56	-1.44	7.20	5.04	43.20*	-41.52	-25.44
DRM	-13.56	-2.40	51.72	64.32	27.84	44.76	.48
RNQ	-1.68	-1.92	-6.60	101.64**	10.80	-69.96	-32.52
DRP	-4.56	-5.04	57.60	42.00	64.68	-33.00	15.48
MII	5.16	-9.12	58.80	114.00****	30.84	58.44	18.96
LSO	-6.84	-.12	-8.52	80.52*	-7.68	23.52	15.12
REF	-15.12	1.92	.60	115.08****	23.40	-12.12	-42.24
DMC	-2.76	-6.36	48.72	115.56****	28.20	51.72	5.04
DRI	-10.08	-6.48	22.44	90.48**	19.92	-30.96	-70.08
MAB	-3.00	-2.04	-18.60	33.00	25.44	-24.60	-15.84
ALX	6.84	-1.56	-3.24	101.36**	15.36	51.48	-51.60
AVERAGE	-6.57	-2.85	19.50	76.76	25.66	6.61	-13.83

[a]Margins are assumed to be 10% of contract value. Model assumptions are such that if a trader invested $1000, $300 (30%) would be used for initial margins and $700 (70%) for potential margin calls. If profits over the period were $100 then the percent return would be 10%.

[b]Significance levels are for the monthly returns within the year and are denoted by * at .10 level, ** at .05 level, *** at .025 level and **** at .01 level.

[c]CHL = Channel
PAR = Parabolic
DRM = Directional Movement
RNQ = Range Quotient
DRP = Directional Parabolic
MII = MII Price Channel

LSO = L-S-O Price Channel
REF = Reference Deviation
DMC = Dual Moving Average Crossover
DRI = Directional Indicator
MAB = Moving Average w/% Price Band
ALX = Alexander's Filter Rule

Table A.15. Annual Returns for Cocoa by Trading Year for All Twelve Systems, 1978-1984.[a,b]

Trading System[c]	Trading Year						
	1978	1979	1980	1981	1982	1983	1984
	(%)						
CHL	18.12	-2.16	12.12	132.24	271.08	-52.56	-338.16
PAR	-11.64	-6.96	-162.60	-32.04	-245.76	-178.08	-132.60
DRM	20.28	-3.24	-28.80	-376.56	21.24	-47.40	-487.92
RNQ	-.60	-25.08	-316.20	-966.24	-58.80	-365.76	-542.64
DRP	9.60	-13.80	-208.68	-367.68	-344.04	-5.04	40.20
MII	12.12	-3.48	58.80	-45.60	-138.72	-28.56	-331.68
LSO	.36	-13.08	-108.72	-228.24	-577.68	-37.56	-642.72
REF	5.76	-1.80	175.44	-53.64	527.88**	-724.32	-691.20
DMC	14.76	-1.44	9.96	-30.36	94.92	-109.32	-487.92
DRI	3.00	-9.48	-201.72	-428.04	-341.40	-524.28	-364.08
MAB	11.52	-8.64	-209.04	-216.48	-338.88	-347.88	-394.68
ALX	14.76	-7.80	-147.24	262.80	-257.16	211.56	-322.56
AVERAGE	8.17	-8.08	-93.89	-200.82	-115.61	-184.10	-391.33

[a]Margins are assumed to be 10% of contract value. Model assumptions are such that if a trader invested $1000, $300 (30%) would be used for initial margins and $700 (70%) for potential margin calls. If profits over the period were $100 then the percent return would be 10%.

[b]Significance levels are for the monthly returns within the year and are denoted by * at .10 level, ** at .05 level, *** at .025 level and **** at .01 level.

[c]CHL = Channel
PAR = Parabolic
DRM = Directional Movement
RNQ = Range Quotient
DRP = Directional Parabolic
MII = MII Price Channel

LSO = L-S-O Price Channel
REF = Reference Deviation
DMC = Dual Moving Average Crossover
DRI = Directional Indicator
MAB = Moving Average w/% Price Band
ALX = Alexander's Filter Rule

Table A.16. Annual Returns for Copper by Trading Year for All Twelve
Systems, 1978-1984.[a,b]

Trading System[c]	Trading Year						
	1978	1979	1980	1981	1982	1983	1984
	(%)						
CHL	-17.52	5.40	40.44	-69.96	-46.80	52.08	28.68
PAR	-22.80	-.72	4.44	-79.80	119.52**	32.04	-48.00
DRM	-2.64	-4.20	72.84	-177.12	-196.68	42.00	10.80
RNQ	-34.68	-2.76	40.68	-29.52	-160.20	-2.40	-123.72
DRP	-19.68	4.08	40.20	-57.12	47.76	21.60	-7.44
MII	-7.20	0.00	3.36	-108.72	-52.44	40.44	-3.24
LSO	-29.28	.36	-177.60	1.08	-162.84	.84	-29.64
REF	-43.44	-5.16	-51.48	-9.48	-170.28	45.60	-26.76
DMC	-18.12	-7.80	-45.12	40.92	-93.48	3.00	-57.12
DRI	-11.16	-10.08	-208.44	-12.48	-223.68	-49.08	-43.92
MAB	-48.60	-7.80	-68.88	-48.24	-335.64	-15.48	-55.56
ALX	-21.60	10.56	28.44	12.24	-23.40	-28.32	27.84
AVERAGE	-23.06	-1.51	-26.76	-44.85	-108.18	11.86	-27.34

[a]Margins are assumed to be 10% of contract value. Model assumptions
are such that if a trader invested $1000, $300 (30%) would be used for
initial margins and $700 (70%) for potential margin calls. If profits
over the period were $100 then the percent return would be 10%.

[b]Significance levels are for the monthly returns within the year and
are denoted by * at .10 level, ** at .05 level, *** at .025 level and
**** at .01 level.

[c]CHL = Channel   LSO = L-S-O Price Channel
PAR = Parabolic   REF = Reference Deviation
DRM = Directional Movement   DMC = Dual Moving Average Crossover
RNQ = Range Quotient   DRI = Directional Indicator
DRP = Directional Parabolic   MAB = Moving Average w/% Price Band
MII = MII Price Channel   ALX = Alexander's Filter Rule

Table A.17.   Annual Returns for Live Cattle by Trading Year for All
Twelve Systems, 1978-1984.[a,b]

Trading System[c]	Trading Year						
	1978	1979	1980	1981	1982	1983	1984
	(%)						
CHL	17.28	6.84	-38.16	6.24	-10.08	-14.28	-68.52
PAR	-2.52	2.16	-59.28	6.96	-103.32	-64.20	-53.64
DRM	9.60*	5.16*	-64.08	28.80	-92.04	13.68	-66.84
RNQ	10.32	-11.28	-160.68	-20.16	-91.32	-27.96	-159.48
DRP	-5.04	4.32	-23.76	41.88	-143.88	-40.32	-74.16
MII	17.16	10.08	-87.72	-53.16	-54.84	-18.72	-71.28
LSO	.96	-12.96	-80.52	4.80	-36.48	-60.36	-134.88
REF	-6.36	-7.44	-25.08	-48.36	-91.68	-95.64	-150.96
DMC	18.24	1.44	-19.80	10.44	-55.80	5.28	-63.84
DRI	15.72	-16.32	-84.48	-55.32	-146.28	-21.96	-182.16
MAB	-2.52	-10.80	-81.96	-21.84	-88.92	-32.16	-160.56
ALX	23.76*	-3.96	-4.20	-37.80	-25.80	5.16	-69.84
AVERAGE	8.05	-2.73	-60.81	-11.46	-78.37	-29.29	-104.68

[a]Margins are assumed to be 10% of contract value. Model assumptions
are such that if a trader invested $1000, $300 (30%) would be used for
initial margins and $700 (70%) for potential margin calls. If profits
over the period were $100 then the percent return would be 10%.

[b]Significance levels are for the monthly returns within the year and
are denoted by * at .10 level, ** at .05 level, *** at .025 level and
**** at .01 level.

[c]CHL = Channel   LSO = L-S-O Price Channel
 PAR = Parabolic   REF = Reference Deviation
 DRM = Directional Movement   DMC = Dual Moving Average Crossover
 RNQ = Range Quotient   DRI = Directional Indicator
 DRP = Directional Parabolic   MAB = Moving Average w/% Price Band
 MII = MII Price Channel   ALX = Alexander's Filter Rule

Table A.18. Annual Returns for Pork Bellies by Trading Year for All
Twelve Systems, 1978-1984.[a,b]

Trading System[c]	Trading Year						
	1978	1979	1980	1981	1982	1983	1984
	(%)						
CHL	40.32**	-2.04	-28.32	-338.76	-77.76	-32.04	40.80
PAR	-9.00	-7.32	103.08	167.16	-69.60	-92.64	-4.08
DRM	38.64*	1.44	-9.48	-103.68	-10.56	-92.16	-38.64
RNQ	40.08*	-21.24	-287.28	-474.60	-32.52	-149.52	-195.84
DRP	25.56*	5.64	-35.76	27.00	-47.16	-48.48	1.68
MII	34.80*	-14.40	-44.76	89.16	-23.76	3.24	-32.40
LSO	41.28**	-6.36	-286.32	-487.92	-117.48	-55.56	-99.72
REF	42.72**	-8.64	-199.08	-755.76	-8.88	-196.32	-94.92
DMC	36.60*	-18.72	120.72	-335.88	18.96	13.68	-30.00
DRI	28.92	0.00	-349.56	-435.48	-156.84	-26.64	-33.60
MAB	30.60	-33.96	-284.40	-280.32	-294.48	-3.60	-12.48
ALX	36.24*	-12.84	-18.12	-108.84	-19.80	-46.68	-59.52
AVERAGE	32.23	-9.87	-109.94	-253.16	-69.99	-60.56	-46.56

[a]Margins are assumed to be 10% of contract value. Model assumptions are such that if a trader invested $1000, $300 (30%) would be used for initial margins and $700 (70%) for potential margin calls. If profits over the period were $100 then the percent return would be 10%.

[b]Significance levels are for the monthly returns within the year and are denoted by * at .10 level, ** at .05 level, *** at .025 level and **** at .01 level.

[c]CHL = Channel
PAR = Parabolic
DRM = Directional Movement
RNQ = Range Quotient
DRP = Directional Parabolic
MII = MII Price Channel

LSO = L-S-O Price Channel
REF = Reference Deviation
DMC = Dual Moving Average Crossover
DRI = Directional Indicator
MAB = Moving Average w/% Price Band
ALX = Alexander's Filter Rule

-65-

Table A.19. Annual Returns for Lumber by Trading Year for All Twelve Systems, 1978-1984.[a,b]

Trading System[c]	Trading Year						
	1978	1979	1980	1981	1982	1983	1984
	(%)						
CHL	-26.28	6.36	-29.16	124.92*	91.32*	77.76	24.72
PAR	.48	-3.00	-56.16	-62.16	-142.56	-117.12	13.80
DRM	-1.56	-10.44	-58.92	-16.68	-71.64	74.76	44.28
RNQ	-11.64	-5.76	-18.12	154.92*	-94.20	-26.40	-19.08
DRP	-6.00	1.92	-79.20	-138.12	-181.80	-64.08	108.36
MII	-3.72	3.96	-62.88	137.88*	25.92	56.76	30.24
LSO	-43.44	0.00	-163.56	-1.32	-68.64	-32.88	61.56
REF	3.12	-1.56	-183.12	128.04*	-61.68	11.04	-43.66
DMC	3.96	4.68	67.44	62.28	-18.00	39.96	68.28
DRI	-9.24	1.56	-43.20	15.24	-78.36	.84	63.36
MAB	.72	6.00*	-124.80	-119.16	-52.92	25.92	-72.00
ALX	6.48	7.20	-104.88	28.56	48.72	59.64	76.32
AVERAGE	-7.26	.91	-71.38	26.20	-50.32	8.85	29.68

[a]Margins are assumed to be 10% of contract value. Model assumptions are such that if a trader invested $1000, $300 (30%) would be used for initial margins and $700 (70%) for potential margin calls. If profits over the period were $100 then the percent return would be 10%.

[b]Significance levels are for the monthly returns within the year and are denoted by * at .10 level, ** at .05 level, *** at .025 level and **** at .01 level.

[c]CHL = Channel
PAR = Parabolic
DRM = Directional Movement
RNQ = Range Quotient
DRP = Directional Parabolic
MII = MII Price Channel
LSO = L-S-O Price Channel
REF = Reference Deviation
DMC = Dual Moving Average Crossover
DRI = Directional Indicator
MAB = Moving Average w/% Price Band
ALX = Alexander's Filter Rule

Table A.20. Annual Returns for Soybeans by Trading Year for All Twelve Systems, 1978-1984.[a,b]

Trading System[c]	Trading Year						
	1978	1979	1980	1981	1982	1983	1984
	(%)						
CHL	-6.12	-8.16	102.48**	7.44	8.16	15.00	-14.28
PAR	10.32	-1.20	33.00	-39.84	-35.40	-49.80	-39.36
DRM	7.92	-9.48	90.00*	60.00	21.48	45.48	-12.12
RNQ	-21.96	-6.96	-44.76	-12.24	-15.60	-62.04	-125.88
DRP	13.44	-3.24	92.40	2.28	-41.88	-48.12	-105.48
MII	-6.48	-9.00	109.56**	30.84	-20.04	34.20	23.28
LSO	-12.12	-9.12	61.80	71.52	-42.00	-7.32	-181.56
REF	3.48	-.84	15.12	-14.76	-32.40	-41.52	-170.88
DMC	-14.16	3.72	55.44	89.88*	-15.24	-9.72	-51.24
DRI	-33.84	-12.36	118.20**	69.96	-4.44	-80.52	-96.48
MAB	1.08	-2.76	75.48*	-3.72	-2.52	-48.72	-139.44
ALX	-16.80	1.44	46.80	45.36	-24.48	22.08	-2.52
AVERAGE	-6.27	-4.83	62.96	25.56	-17.03	-19.25	-76.33

[a]Margins are assumed to be 10% of contract value. Model assumptions are such that if a trader invested $1000, $300 (30%) would be used for initial margins and $700 (70%) for potential margin calls. If profits over the period were $100 then the percent return would be 10%.

[b]Significance levels are for the monthly returns within the year and are denoted by * at .10 level, ** at .05 level, *** at .025 level and **** at .01 level.

[c]CHL = Channel
PAR = Parabolic
DRM = Directional Movement
RNQ = Range Quotient
DRP = Directional Parabolic
MII = MII Price Channel

LSO = L-S-O Price Channel
REF = Reference Deviation
DMC = Dual Moving Average Crossover
DRI = Directional Indicator
MAB = Moving Average w/% Price Band
ALX = Alexander's Filter Rule

Table A.21. Annual Returns for Silver by Trading Year for All Twelve Systems, 1978-1984.[a,b]

Trading System[c]	Trading Year						
	1978	1979	1980	1981	1982	1983	1984
	(%)						
CHL	-17.40	26.16	69.96	98.52	50.04	94.92	120.72*
PAR	4.32	23.16	268.68	-46.80	190.32**	-27.96	-12.72
DRM	-26.52	36.48*	-98.40	-81.48	123.48**	105.12	60.12
RNQ	6.84	25.68	-3.72	-24.48	155.76*	-186.60	-60.96
DRP	-12.00	35.04*	149.76	-18.96	257.52*	106.32	123.72
MII	-25.08	46.68***	-7.08	3.96	-152.88	-58.44	92.88
LSO	-7.80	45.72**	38.04	-123.00	-78.60	106.56	-116.16
REF	-19.56	46.32**	-3.60	-43.92	-415.08	-52.08	-19.08
DMC	-6.48	50.28***	55.68	84.96	118.92	-55.80	-1.80
DRI	-83.76	47.52***	-2.40	19.92	-313.68	-122.16	71.16
MAB	-16.44	32.04*	-6.24	42.00	-18.60	-99.72	85.80
ALX	3.84	50.88***	322.32**	13.20	143.52**	-57.00	-35.40
AVERAGE	-16.67	38.83	65.25	-6.34	5.06	-20.57	25.69

[a]Margins are assumed to be 10% of contract value. Model assumptions are such that if a trader invested $1000, $300 (30%) would be used for initial margins and $700 (70%) for potential margin calls. If profits over the period were $100 then the percent return would be 10%.

[b]Significance levels are for the monthly returns within the year and are denoted by * at .10 level, ** at .05 level, *** at .025 level and **** at .01 level.

[c]CHL = Channel   LSO = L-S-O Price Channel
PAR = Parabolic   REF = Reference Deviation
DRM = Directional Movement   DMC = Dual Moving Average Crossover
RNQ = Range Quotient   DRI = Directional Indicator
DRP = Directional Parabolic MAB = Moving Average w/% Price Band
MII = MII Price Channel   ALX = Alexander's Filter Rule

Table A.22.   Annual Returns for Sugar by Trading Year for All Twelve
Systems, 1978-1984.[a,b]

Trading System[c]	Trading Year						
	1978	1979	1980	1981	1982	1983	1984
	(%)						
CHL	-3.60	10.08	83.52	193.08*	130.32	122.04	167.40*
PAR	-14.64	-10.08	238.20*	37.08	111.00	49.68	-14.16
DRM	-16.80	4.56	199.08	-55.56	56.52	16.32	135.84
RNQ	6.48	.48	28.20	-151.08	-84.00	137.04	12.72
DRP	-23.88	-.96	351.54*	115.44	55.56	-22.44	11.52
MII	-18.00	8.76	235.80	42.36	-8.88	45.96	78.36
LSO	-34.80	5.88	299.52	-112.80	-74.28	-70.32	42.00
REF	4.68	8.28	-198.00	-57.00	-167.28	-76.08	105.00
DMC	7.20	12.60	122.40	70.80	-7.44	135.12	193.68**
DRI	-27.72	-4.08	156.36	59.52	-91.92	-84.12	102.48
MAB	11.28	8.40	119.28	108.48	-16.68	-206.16	8.88
ALX	-2.88	15.24	247.80	35.76	19.68	19.44	119.04
AVERAGE	-9.39	4.93	157.00	23.84	-6.45	5.54	80.23

[a]Margins are assumed to be 10% of contract value. Model assumptions
are such that if a trader invested $1000, $300 (30%) would be used for
initial margins and $700 (70%) for potential margin calls. If profits
over the period were $100 then the percent return would be 10%.

[b]Significance levels are for the monthly returns within the year and
are denoted by * at .10 level, ** at .05 level, *** at .025 level and
**** at .01 level.

[c]CHL = Channel   LSO = L-S-O Price Channel
PAR = Parabolic   REF = Reference Deviation
DRM = Directional Movement   DMC = Dual Moving Average Crossover
RNQ = Range Quotient   DRI = Directional Indicator
DRP = Directional Parabolic   MAB = Moving Average w/% Price Band
MII = MII Price Channel   ALX = Alexander's Filter Rule

Table A.23. Annual Returns for Treasury Bills by Trading Year for All
Twelve Systems, 1978-1984.[a,b]

Trading System[c]	Trading Year						
	1978	1979	1980	1981	1982	1983	1984
				(%)			
CHL	NA	5.88	587.16*	-65.52	-43.80	-60.36	228.84***
PAR	NA	21.84*	211.68	228.12	-207.60	-54.72	91.80
DRM	NA	3.84	823.80***	105.24	-250.80	-79.44	193.32*
RNQ	NA	-20.16	667.20**	-429.24	62.40	-528.48	7.68
DRP	NA	35.76**	558.84	504.84	134.76	-128.40	247.08**
MII	NA	8.16	810.12****	111.60	153.84	-106.92	162.72
LSO	NA	-14.28	883.44*	-18.24	476.40****	-242.88	246.00***
REF	NA	-7.92	1124.48*	-366.24	536.88*	-161.04	308.52***
DMC	NA	-12.60	517.68**	-59.88	128.52	-66.24	259.32**
DRI	NA	-5.64	1202.88***	559.68	-55.20	-379.32	32.04
MAB	NA	-25.68	489.96**	-741.96	151.68	-43.20	96.84**
ALX	NA	-20.52	659.52*	-552.12	96.96	-160.32	173.76
AVERAGE	NA	-2.61	711.40	-60.31	98.67	-167.61	170.66

[a]Margins are assumed to be 5% of contract value. Model assumptions
are such that if a trader invested $1000, $300 (30%) would be used for
initial margins and $700 (70%) for potential margin calls. If profits
over the period were $100 then the percent return would be 10%.

[b]Significance levels are for the monthly returns within the year and
are denoted by * at .10 level, ** at .05 level, *** at .025 level and
**** at .01 level.

[c]CHL = Channel   LSO = L-S-O Price Channel
PAR = Parabolic   REF = Reference Deviation
DRM = Directional Movement   DMC = Dual Moving Average Crossover
RNQ = Range Quotient   DRI = Directional Indicator
DRP = Directional Parabolic   MAB = Moving Average w/% Price Band
MII = MII Price Channel   ALX = Alexander's Filter Rule

Table A.24. Annual Returns for British Pound by Trading Year for All
Twelve Systems, 1978-1984.[a,b]

Trading System[c]	Trading Year						
	1978	1979	1980	1981	1982	1983	1984
				(%)			
CHL	NA	NA	67.92**	19.80	-88.44	-64.92	48.24
PAR	NA	NA	-9.84	107.04*	-50.64	-17.64	11.40
DRM	NA	NA	34.20	35.04	12.60	13.44	8.52
RNQ	NA	NA	-77.28	-61.80	29.76	-34.92	-36.24
DRP	NA	NA	34.32	95.88	-33.96	-17.88	73.44
MII	NA	NA	9.48	102.00*	-147.36	-13.20	58.44
LSO	NA	NA	-25.20	-60.72	43.80	-24.84	27.84
REF	NA	NA	-87.12	78.36	33.36	-14.76	7.68
DMC	NA	NA	40.20	-40.32	23.76	36.60	69.00
DRI	NA	NA	-70.44	-98.76	57.00*	8.88	52.44
MAB	NA	NA	-12.12	-111.96	-121.68	-116.16	33.24
ALX	NA	NA	54.96*	-78.60	-51.60	-117.24	-6.72
AVERAGE	NA	NA	-3.41	-1.17	-24.45	-30.22	28.94

[a]Margins are assumed to be 5% of contract value. Model assumptions are such that if a trader invested $1000, $300 (30%) would be used for initial margins and $700 (70%) for potential margin calls. If profits over the period were $100 then the percent return would be 10%.

[b]Significance levels are for the monthly returns within the year and are denoted by * at .10 level, ** at .05 level, *** at .025 level and **** at .01 level.

[c]CHL = Channel   LSO = L-S-O Price Channel
PAR = Parabolic   REF = Reference Deviation
DRM = Directional Movement   DMC = Dual Moving Average Crossover
RNQ = Range Quotient   DRI = Directional Indicator
DRP = Directional Parabolic   MAB = Moving Average w/% Price Band
MII = MII Price Channel   ALX = Alexander's Filter Rule

Table A.25.   Annual Returns for Duetsch Mark by Trading Year for All
Twelve Systems, 1978-1984.[a,b]

Trading System[c]	Trading Year						
	1978	1979	1980	1981	1982	1983	1984
				(%)			
CHL	NA	NA	87.00*	95.88	29.40	38.88	81.12
PAR	NA	NA	75.00	68.04	10.08	36.96	-13.08
DRM	NA	NA	93.84*	138.72**	85.92**	-42.36	64.68
RNQ	NA	NA	64.20	87.60	-97.08	-35.16	74.64
DRP	NA	NA	137.04	113.64	71.16	29.16	39.24
MII	NA	NA	74.40	139.44**	20.04	23.88	58.56
LSO	NA	NA	36.36	27.36	-15.84	-50.52	98.76
REF	NA	NA	65.76	6.00	-150.72	2.64	-12.48
DMC	NA	NA	62.28	61.92	51.72	-21.60	77.16
DRI	NA	NA	15.72	37.82	38.28	46.32	61.20
MAB	NA	NA	39.00	-12.84	-.24	-78.72	85.56*
ALX	NA	NA	-90.24	-134.88	-19.92	16.44	-21.12
AVERAGE	NA	NA	55.03	52.40	1.90	-2.84	49.52

[a]Margins are assumed to be 5% of contract value. Model assumptions are
such that if a trader invested $1000, $300 (30%) would be used for
initial margins and $700 (70%) for potential margin calls. If profits
over the period were $100 then the percent return would be 10%.

[b]Significance levels are for the monthly returns within the year and
are denoted by * at .10 level, ** at .05 level, *** at .025 level and
**** at .01 level.

[c]CHL = Channel   LSO = L-S-O Price Channel
PAR = Parabolic   REF = Reference Deviation
DRM = Directional Movement   DMC = Dual Moving Average Crossover
RNQ = Range Quotient   DRI = Directional Indicator
DRP = Directional Parabolic   MAB = Moving Average w/% Price Band
MII = MII Price Channel   ALX = Alexander's Filter Rule

Partial List of Publications of Traders Press, Inc.®

7 Secrets Every Commodity Trader Needs to Know (Mound)
A Complete Guide to Trading Profits (Paris)
A Professional Look at S&P Day Trading (Trivette)
A Treasury of Wall Street Wisdom (Editors: Schultz & Coslow)
Beginner's Guide to Computer Assisted Trading (Alexander)
Channels and Cycles: A Tribute to J.M. Hurst (Millard)
Chart Reading for Professional Traders (Jenkins)
Commodity Spreads: Analysis, Selection and Trading Techniques (Smith)
Comparison of Twelve Technical Trading Systems (Lukac, Brorsen, & Irwin)
Complete Stock Market Trading and Forecasting Course (Jenkins)
Cyclic Analysis (J.M. Hurst)
Dynamic Trading (Miner)
Essentials of Trading: It's Not WHAT You Think, It's HOW You Think (Pesavento)
Exceptional Trading: The Mind Game (Roosevelt)
Fibonacci Ratios with Pattern Recognition (Pesavento)
Futures Spread Trading: The Complete Guide (Smith)
Geometry of Markets (Gilmore)
Geometry of Stock Market Profits (Jenkins)
Harmonic Vibrations (Pesavento)
How to Trade in Stocks (Livermore & Smitten)
Hurst Cycles Course (J.M. Hurst)
Investing by the Stars (Weingarten)
Investor Skills Training: Managing Emotions and Risk in the Market (Ronin)
It's Your Option (Zelkin)
Magic of Moving Averages (Lowry)
Market Beaters (Collins)
Market Rap: The Odyssey of a Still-Struggling Commodity Trader (Collins)
Overcoming 7 Deadly Sins of Trading (Roosevelt)
Planetary Harmonics of Speculative Markets (Pesavento)
Point & Figure Charting (Aby)
Point & Figure Charting: Commodity and Stock Trading Techniques (Zieg)
Precision Trading with Stevenson Price and Time Targets (J.R. Stevenson)
Private Thoughts From a Trader's Diary (Pesavento & MacKay)
Profitable Patterns for Stock Trading (Pesavento)
RoadMap to the Markets (Busby)
RSI: The Complete Guide (Hayden)
Stock Patterns for Day Trading (2 volumes) (Rudd)
Technically Speaking (Wilkinson)
Technical Trading Systems for Commodities and Stocks (Patel)
The Amazing Life of Jesse Livermore: World's Greatest Stock Trader (Smitten)
The Handbook of Global Securities Operations (O'Connell & Steiniger)
The Opening Price Principle: The Best Kept Secret on Wall Street (Pesavento & MacKay)
The Professional Commodity Trader (Kroll)
The Taylor Trading Technique (Taylor)
The Trading Rule That Can Make You Rich* (Dobson)
Top Traders Under Fire (Collins)
Trading Secrets of the Inner Circle (Goodwin)
Trading S&P Futures and Options (Lloyd)
Twelve Habitudes of Highly Successful Traders (Roosevelt)
Understanding Bollinger Bands (Dobson)
Understanding Eminis: Trading to Win (Williams)
Understanding Fibonacci Numbers (Dobson)
Winning Edge 4 (Toghraie)
Winning Market Systems (Appel)

Please contact Traders Press to receive our current catalog describing these and many other books and gifts of interest to investors and traders.
800-927-8222 ~ 864-298-0222 ~ fax 864-298-0221
http://www.traderspress.com ~ e-mail ~ customerservice@traderspress.com